Knowing His Word: Real Faith for the End Times

You Shall Know the Truth, and The Truth Shall Set You Free

Melvin Zelaya

KNOWING HIS WORD: REAL FAITH FOR THE END TIMES

You Shall Know the Truth, and The Truth Shall Set You Free

Copyright © 2025 by Melvin Zelaya.

ISBN 979-8-89672-215-1 (paperback)
ISBN 979-8-89672-216-8 (ebook)

Printed in the United States of America.

PROMINENT
BOOKS

5830 E 2nd St, Ste 7000 #9983
Casper, Wyoming, 82609
USA

Contents

Foreword

The Genesis of the Inquiry

What you are poised to explore in this narrative may well encapsulate the ultimate synthesis of every existential question that has reverberated within me since I was seven, navigating the corridors of elementary school. In those tranquil interludes of youth, I found myself grappling with life's mysteries—the uncertainties of our existence, the mechanisms, and rationales behind our presence in this great circle we call earth, and, most crucially, the purpose that would define my journey on it. I speculate that many of you harbor a parallel curiosity threading through the fabric of your own life narrative.

For years, I delved into Greek and Roman mythology, never pausing to interrogate why these civilizations bestowed such majestic titles upon their gods—Zeus, Apollo, Jupiter—mirroring the celestial array adorning our night sky. It escaped my notice that this constituted the breadth of their religious existence, spanning from the scattering of humanity at Babel, to Abraham's era, when the authentic God forsook such grandiose epithets for the unpretentious title of what Christians have come to know as "The Father."

A Significant Word Unexamined

The profundity of that Name eluded me—it lingered as a mere term, devoid of any personal resonance, significance, or relation to me, personally. I failed to ponder its deeper connotations—a guardian, protector, sustainer, and advocate for His lineage—perhaps due to the absence of a tangible paternal figure in my own life. Circumstances beyond my father's control dictated him to work in a distant town to support our family, severing any substantive connection with him. We all recognize the familial construct—a mosaic of distinct individuals—and later, as a father myself, I sought to discern the unique temperaments and talents of my daughters, tailoring my approach to their singularities. Yet, despite our earnest endeavors, they often perceive fathers as having a "favorite," a misconception far removed from reality, but not sure about sons, since I lack experience in that department.

Divine Dilemma

My assertion here is that God, the architect of all creation, confronts a comparable conundrum with each child He adopts through His Son's redemptive sacrifice—when one opts for Him to bear the cross we merit, thus bridging the divide we all have from our True Father. This work is explicitly crafted for those prepared to acknowledge His existence as an incontrovertible truth, not a speculative theory, or a religious edifice, as **2 Timothy 3:5** labels and critiques as those clinging to:

> "an outward veneer of piety [religion], while renouncing its *transformative* power [as their *actions deny* their faith claims]."

Awakening to Truth

I arrived at a pivotal juncture where, through studying astronomy, cosmology, and mathematics, and marveling at the universe's intricate design, I recognized the deception pervading academia's humanist creeds. Elemental logic and pragmatism dismantled the notion that a primordial broth could orchestrate—among myriad of wonders—the symbiotic equilibrium where vegetation trades oxygen for our carbon dioxide exhalations, or that a luminous intellect engineered the transfer of trillions of gallons of seawater as rainfall to sustain this cycle. Even more astonishing, such feats are trivial compared to the exacting tolerances governing the choreography of stars, galaxies, and the natural realm enveloping this cosmos.

Looking for Love in All the Wrong Places

When I first became aware that what I have heard in colleges and universities and even in Time Magazine, with the caption "Is God Dead?" several decades ago, was nothing more than the humanist's religion propaganda—I just made a simple prayer into the air (so I thought). I didn't really knew what to say while I was watching a beautiful cloudy, end of day sunset, which screamed creation and verbalized what was inside me. I just blurted, "God, if you are real, I want to know You." I won't bore you with the details but exactly 24 hours later, two young Mormon missionaries were knocking at my door, and wrongly assumed that this was a "sign" from God answering my prayer. There is no doubt that this has happened to millions of others when they are seeking for God, and end up, as the saying goes, "catching religion," and certainly, I did just that.

It's Easy to Prove God's Existence

Although I would not know about an amazing preacher by the name of Ray Comfort for another 47 years, he nails it when somebody asked him if he could prove the existence of God. His response was quick, "yes I can, when you see a beautiful painting or a skyscraper, you do not 'need proof' to know whether that painting has a painter as its **creator**, nor that of a **builder** who designed and built the high-rise building, so, when you see the amazing beauty and complexity of Nature, any rational person does not need, nor asks for "proof" to know that both of these creations, **has** a Creator." That is exactly what I saw on that beautiful Summer day back in 1975.

A Quest for the Real

Upon encountering this Real God, I embarked on an odyssey to assimilate all I could in order to know all about Him and on how, I could get closer to Him. Once I discovered the solutions to this task, during the last fifty years or so of searching, every query I had from those nascent days—and the subsequent questions they spawned in my mind and I am here to testify that all of them have been answered and resolved, by understanding His Word through His Spirit.

Religion's Shortfall

Though imbued with noble intent, each religion that I investigated, embraced, or practiced, failed to fulfill the destiny He ordains for those He summons. From that precipice, I forged a new path to seek Him as He envisioned, fostering in the end, an authentic Father-son communion. Akin to human family, He engages us according to our distinctiveness and the aspirations He perceives within our hearts, exemplifying impartiality and addressing us equitably in our uniqueness, liberating us from envy or rancor toward one another.

An Invitation, Not a Mandate

In this work, you *will not find* a **single quotation** from any "*Bible Scholar*, **theologian**, or a *religious philosopher*," because their ideas, interpretations, and conclusions are derived in the flesh—through their intellect, life experiences, and their rearing culture. This is why, if you put ten of them in a group together, you'll have *ten opinions* on any biblical topic discussed. Unfortunately, these people, such as theologians, teachers, pastors, and preachers as well, are taken seriously, as if they actually possess an *accurate knowledge* of God's oracles.

So, what this narrative is about to embark on is to *question centuries old beliefs and traditions* which,, as far as I know, are still unknown in religious circles and have never been expounded on, discussed, preached, or written about that I know of. All the quotations you will find here comes 100% from the Word of God. Why, might one ask? Simply because God has established in **Luke 1:4**; **John 1:14-17**; and many others, that there is **only ONE Truth** and in **John 17:17**, we find that this Truth **is** the Written, and Living Word, Christ Jesus. At the same time, this exposition **does not** aim to "*persuade or proselytize*" anyone into **any** religion, or with a new "*doctrine*," for each one of us must navigate their own trajectory within His redemptive blueprint for fallen humanity, as this work will elucidate.

Like our mortal parents, He, in His Word has merely extended only *an invitation* to receive His finest reward for those who love Him as expressed in **1 Corinthians 2:9**. However, this gift is available *only* to those willing to embrace His plan of salvation *as it's designed* and **obey** Him—not different than a human parent offering their children, in the best way they can, simply because they love them. Nevertheless, more often than not, they are ignored and rejected, and again, a normal loving parent accepts that too, and would never hate, scorn, forsake, or resent His children for failing to heed and obey them.

Please bear this in mind that as you read—that this narrative is merely an articulation of what He has already written in His Word, expressing a Divine Father's longing for each one of His treasured children *to opt-in* into the best He has to offer **to all of us**—but, this is only predicated if are able to discern the value of what He is offering, and are willing to accept His *terms and conditions* to receive it.

With that, let us commence.

αΣΩ

Chapter One

The Faith God is Looking For

A World Gone Mad

The world today teeters on a precipice: wars loom with the potential to escalate into a cataclysmic Third World War, instilling dread in every heart. Yet beneath this tumult lies a spiritual undercurrent. For those versed in the prophetic tapestry of Scripture—spanning the New Testament and Jewish writings—these events align with an inevitable trajectory that most people do not wish for, or dare to think about it. We are powerless to halt or modify this tide. As a Christian, I perceive what's coming in the imminent horizon; if you share this vantage point as well, you might wonder: Do I *possess* a robust faith in God in order to navigate what's lies just ahead of us? Jesus assures us in **Revelation 3:10** that He will shield us from the severe trials to come. These events are certain to unfold:

> "Because you have kept the Word of My endurance [My command to persevere], I **will** keep you [*safe*], from the hour of trial, that hour, which is about to come on the whole [inhabited] world to test, those who live on the earth."

The Facade of Human Faith

Pose this question in any church: "Amidst the chaos engulfing the earth, who believes their faith is strong enough that will sustain them?" Every hand would rise, undoubtedly. But how do we ascertain whether our faith is genuinely authentic and aligned with God's standard? This dilemma spurred my introspection. In **Luke 18:8**, Jesus poses a haunting query:

> "When the Son of Man returns, will He *find* this faith [of a tenacious caliber] on the earth?" (**Greek Amplified Bible**, utilized throughout this work).

He wouldn't voice this unless it bore profound weight—a clarion call to heed. We must discern whether we have the faith He seeks, evaluate it and decide whether we possess it to be spared from what is coming, and, if lacking, determine how to attain it. Years of contemplation led me to clarity; may the verses herein illuminate your path as they did mine.

A Divine Inquiry

I am convinced our Lord framed this question for today's Christians with deliberate intent, signaling a vital truth demanding our attention. It becomes imperative not merely to comprehend the ***nature*** of the faith He describes, but to juxtapose it against the faith we presume to hold. Once we confront this honestly, we might ask: *Does it meet His expectations?* Should it fall short, how might we acquire it? Decades of seeking yielded an answer that satisfied me, and I urge you to scrutinize each passage cited in this discourse, hoping they crystallize for you as they have for me.

A Sobering Revelation

After decades immersed in His Word, I must concede a humbling truth: the faith I uncovered revealed that I lacked the caliber He desires. Until that epiphany, my perceived "faith" was self-generated—originating and terminating within me. It was a construct of my intellect, interwoven with notions peddled as "God's Word" by religious individuals, "biblical experts," books, or tapes dictating what "faith" is, or is supposed to be.

In truth, I was clueless myself as to the kind of faith He required. Years of pursuit unveiled that only His Spirit can birth, nurture, and manifest the faith of **Romans 12:3** within us—provided we obey His Word in John **14:26** and in **16:13**.

This is the chaff that Satan has deftly scattered into the religious system, explaining why Christian's grapple not only to define faith, but to personify it—because we fail to let His Spirit plant the good seed in us (**Matthew 13:3; Mark 4:3**). What surprised me is that I was looking for something that I already had, and given to me in **Romans 12:3**:

> "For **by the grace** [of God] given to me, I say to every one of you not to think more highly of himself [and of his importance and ability] than he ought to think; but to think so as to have sound judgment, **as God has __apportioned__ to __each__, a degree of faith** [and a **purpose**, *designed for service*]."

Faith vs. Belief

Scrutinize this passage on biblical faith per His Word above, and it dawns on us that, what we perceive as "faith," often amounts to a mere *personal belief* in something or someone—any entity or ideal. This is deep-seated, and intrinsic to human nature. Yet, as I will substantiate biblically later, it diverges from the faith God delineates in the above cited Scripture. Personal faith hinges on our own human capacity, or on the external teachings from religious "gurus" or purveyors of religion—entirely earthly in scope—rather than a faith anchored solely in the one that God has *already given* to us to use, as this work will disclose. My former faith rested on believing in things or people—commonplace, yes, but not the faith God imparts per **Romans 12:3**. His faith flows from Himself, *not us*—a truth absent from any church teaching that I've ever known.

Let's revisit **Romans 12:3**—God grants a "*__measure__* of faith for a *purpose* and designed for *service*."

What purpose? What service? He elucidates this in **Acts 26:16-18**:

"Get up and stand on your feet. I have appeared to you for this **purpose**, to appoint you [to serve] as a minister and as a witness [to testify, with authority,] not only to the things which you have seen, but also to the things in which I will appear to you, [choosing you for Myself and] rescuing you from the Jewish people and from the Gentiles, *to whom I am sending* you, to *open* their [spiritual] eyes so that they may turn from darkness to light and from the power of Satan to God, that they *may receive forgiveness* and release from their sins (do notice that salvation comes **through** our **belief** in the message) **AND** an **inheritance** among **those** (some, not **all**) who have been *sanctified* (set apart, made holy) by **faith** in Me'."

Can you see the distinction expressed above? *Belief* secures salvation; but *only His faith* bestows to us His inheritance, *reserved* only for those who wield it. Conflate them, and clarity dissolves. Again, As we can readily notice too, is that the text **differentiates** our belief from that of faith where, salvation comes by our **believing** the *salvation* message, and the *inheritance* **through faith** in Jesus, **not** by your belief in Him—the same **difference** between a believer, and a disciple. Any other explanation would be illogical.

Trust in the Source

This delineation between belief (for salvation) and the inheritance of God's Kingdom (faith in Jesus *alone*, **not** a religion or church) is stark—His declaration, not mine. I must reiterate: this faith *originates* from Him, not us, bearing a deliberate purpose which is foreign to the rigid tenets of organized religion's dogmas.

James 1:17 reinforces this truth:

"Every good thing given and every **perfect** gift is *from* above; it comes down from the Father of lights [the Creator and Sustainer of the heavens], in whom there is no variation [no rising or setting] or shadow cast by His turning [for He is perfect and *never changes*]."

Thus, contrary to church rhetoric, we cannot "***seek***, ***add*** to it, or ***cultivate***" this faith—it is already **flawless** because it's coming *from* Him, not us.

He rebuked His disciples for lacking faith even as small as a mustard seed. What—or Who—is that faith? In **Luke 8:25**, after stilling the storm, He asked:

> "And He said to them, 'Where is **your** faith [your **confidence** in Me]?' They were afraid and astonished, saying to one another, 'Who then is this, that He commands even the winds and the sea, and they obey Him'?"

They were gripped by fear and awe, marveling, "Who is this?" They succumbed to dread, not faith. Jesus **is our faith**—our trust in Him—the antithesis of **fear**. He stood before them as faith incarnate, and so He does for us today. Contrast this with today's church teachings—faith is not so convoluted, is it? Grasping this dichotomy within salvation's framework clarifies why we've conflated our human ***belief***, with that of God's freely given ***faith*** of **Romans 12:3**.

It is quite obvious then why ***anybody*** can be saved since we, as unregenerate human beings, are **not born** possessing His faith, but once saved, the opportunity to receive an inheritance is now ***open to anyone*** as well. This logical conclusion is not rocket science once common sense has its way.

As this work centers solely on this divine faith requisite for claiming His inheritance—which will be proven biblically—we'll sideline human belief, which is meaningless in this quest (see **John 6:63**), and pursue the ***eternal faith*** of God.

It is also crucial to understand as well that, this faith that comes from God is ***totally independent*** from our ***salvation***, therefore, it's also central to understand then that, this faith from God, being autonomous from our salvation, means that to get His faith, one must be saved ***first***.

This is illustrated in the most famous Gospel passage of **John 3:16**:

> "For God so [greatly] loved and dearly prized the world, that He [even] gave His [One and] **only** begotten Son, so that **whoever believes** (notice that *no mention of faith* is found here) in Him [**as Savior**] shall not perish but have eternal life."
> (It's on the *basis of* **belief**, *not faith* as confirmed in **Acts 2:21**, and **Rom. 10:13** plus many others).

As we can see here, **no** mention at all, nor in the entire four gospels, where *entering* the kingdom of God is neither implied, nor connected to the state of being saved.

A Redemptive Blueprint

Yet, discerning this distinction between salvation and an inheritance—and it's sequence in God's redemptive schema, conceived from the foundation of the world (**Matthew 13:35**; and in **25:34**; **Ephesians 1:4**)—is paramount to discern. All of this will unfold through the biblical evidence that will be presented ahead.

Having clarified His plan, this book explores acquiring that divine faith that *grants* this inheritance of the kingdom, but only to those who possess it which, in simple terms means to believe the promise of **Romans 12:3**, just the same as you believed in Christ Jesus (see **Rom. 6:4**)—this is how my human faith was transformed into His. If your faith wavers, journey with me. Jesus posed that question in **Luke 18:8** because it matters—profoundly—to Him and to *us*.

Scripture's Wake-Up Call

He exhorts us in **2 Corinthians 13:5**:

> "**Test** *and* **evaluate** yourselves *to see* whether **you** are in the *faith and living your lives* as [committed] believers. Examine yourselves [not me]! Or do you not recognize this about yourselves

[by an *ongoing **experience***] that Jesus Christ **is in you**—unless indeed you **fail** the test and are **rejected** as **counterfeit**?"

What exactly does He mean by, "to be rejected"? **Hosea 4:6** elucidates:

"My people are destroyed for **lack of knowledge** [of My law (our Bible), where I **unveil** My will]. Because **you** [the priestly nation (see **1 Cor. 4:8**; **Revelation 5:10**)] spurned knowledge (of His Word and will), I too will **reject you** from being My priests."

Can you now grasp why possessing and wielding *His faith* (not ours) is vital? However, as I started to immerse myself into His Word, I was unnerved when I read several passages in the Gospels, such as this one in **Matt. 25:11-12**:

"Later the others also came, and said, 'Lord, Lord, open [the door] for us.' But He replied, 'I assure you and most solemnly say to you, I **do not know you** [*we have **NO** relationship*]."

These are "Christian" people that He is talking to, not pagans, and do not overlook what is the **consequence** for *not knowing* Him (by His Word *through* His Spirit) and it does *not* mean to be consigned to *damnation*, but only being **barred** (by **your** *own choice*, per **Hosea 4:6**) from **being** in *His Presence* as His priest.

For decades, trying to decipher these sayings from our Lord, became my own Ahab's white whale for me, while trying to explain away a disturbing feeling that these two passages mentioned above could very well *apply* to me also.

A Growing Concern

My unease swelled into palpable apprehension when I encountered **Matthew 7:21-23** piercing even deeper:

"Not everyone who says to Me, 'Lord, Lord,' will **enter *the kingdom of heaven*** (something that it's *independent* from our salvation), but only he who **does the will** of My Father (as written in His Word) who is in heaven. Many will say to Me on that day [when I *judge* them], 'Lord, Lord, have we not prophesied in Your name, and driven out demons in Your name, and done many miracles in Your name?' And then I will declare to them publicly, 'I **never knew you**; depart from Me [you are **banished** from **My presence**], you who act in lawlessness' [**disregarding My commands**]."

A Stagnant Faith

In my experience, the only thing that changed in my daily life after I was saved was going to church on Sundays and meetings on Wednesdays and helping out with church things. But I was later frightened to realize that, as a baby Christian, I neither saw, considered, or even knew if something was amiss in my walk with Him—missing what **Revelation 2:4** cautions us about:

> "But I have this [charge] against you, that *you have left* your first love [you have lost the depth of love that you *first had* for Me]."

Yet, by God's grace, this dread and concern, began to subside when I began immersing myself in Scripture *firsthand*, rather than from a third party's opinion or point of view. It took many years for me to come to the realization that the *only way* to know Him, was to **know** His Word taught directly from Him where, once I understood it for myself, and became proficient in its content, it brought me to the place of fully perceiving, what **John 8:31-32** is *really saying* to us:

> "So, Jesus was saying to the Jews who had believed Him, '**IF you abide in My Word** [continually *obeying* My teachings and **living** in *accordance with them*, **then** (and only then)] *you are* **truly My disciples**. And you **will know** the truth, and the truth will set you **free**."

Unveiling True Faith

It wasn't until I embraced His Word as my life's handbook, if you will, did I start forging a deeper bond with Jesus, aspiring to emulate Him, trying to follow in His steps (**1 Corinthians 4:16; 11:1-3**), adhering to His precepts and living as He intends me to live, to the best of *my capacity* since, believe it or not, He knows we are not perfect. Guided by the Holy Spirit, I realized that *nothing* could come from me—He supplies it **all**, as promised in **John 14:26** and **16:13**. Trust me, this isn't as daunting as it seems.

Therefore, my voluntary decision to apprise and familiarize myself with His Word, the owner's manual if you will, was my own starting point of truly beginning to know **the Person** of Jesus Christ, and the many facets of His Character, Will, Values, and His *expectations from me*, that encouraged me to try and start, *imitating* Him, (**1 Cor. 4:16; 11:1-3;**), and obeying His commandments and His way of *doing things* in my daily life as He modeled it Himself while He lived on this earth the *best way I know how*. It was at this junction that I understood what **2 John 1:5** is saying to *all of us*:

> "Now I ask you, lady, *not* as if I were *writing* to you a **new commandment**, but [simply reminding you of] the **one** which we have had from the beginning, that we **love** and unselfishly **seek the best** for one another."

In another words, what He wants out of us is not complicated at all! It's a matter of obeying **Matt. 22:39-40**:

> "The second is like it, 'You shall love your neighbor as yourself [that is, unselfishly seek the **best or higher** good for others].' The **whole Law** and the [writings of the] Prophets **depend** on these two commandments."

Imagine that! What the **Christian religion** has made rocket science, is no simpler than He, requiring me that I love Him eternally as *my first love*, and to **treat others** the way *I would like* to be treated myself. How right He was when He said in **Matt. 11:25**:

"I praise You, Father, Lord of heaven and earth [I openly and joyfully acknowledge Your great wisdom], that You have **hidden** these things [these **spiritual** truths (that **only** the Holy Spirit is able to do] from the wise and intelligent and **revealed** them to infants [to new believers, to those *seeking God's will and purpose*]."

Trust me, being a **real Christian**, is **not** as overwhelming as the religious establishment has made it to be in order to be *relevant outside* of God's **Eph. 4:11** call.

This is by no means, a criticism, but an observation that might explain their failure to produce disciples, rather than believers.

This might also explain why most Christians will strive to memorize **John 3:16**, which is fine, however, a disciple would understand that it was more important for us to memorize the whole chapter of **1 Corinthians 13**, since that section of scripture is the necessary foundation to **fulfill** His Second Command of **Matt. 22:39-40** cited before.

Stagnation at the Start

Of course, initially, my mindset had been shaped by the doctrines and set of guidelines being uttered in the churches I had attended and, I had assumed through them that, I had to exert whatever "faith" I had to manufacture on my own. But, to me, it turned out to be no more than mere wishful thinking—hopes akin to Napoleon Hill's *Think and Grow Rich*—no distinction there. Don't misunderstand: our thoughts **do** *wield power* to change a life—a faculty God instilled (**Proverbs 23:7**) in us, and operative for all human beings, Christian or otherwise.

Yet His faith, per **Romans 12:3**, is a divine gift to be pursued relentlessly (**Proverbs 25:2; Matthew 6:33, 7:7**) until He reveals it, and implements it in us. He does it *all* (**Psalm 127:1; Zech. 4:6**)— now, I yearn to impart this information to others.

Pursuing Hidden Treasures

Now, why do I mention this? Well, for those who profess Him as savior, and desire to find, and use this **Roman 12:3** faith, it is one of those mysteries where **Proverbs 25:2** encourages us to *seek and find* (**Matt. 6:33** and **7:7**), and many others:

> "It is the glory of God to *conceal* a matter, but the glory of **kings** (us, see **1 Cor. 4:8**; **Rev. 5:10**) is to **search** out the matter."

If one does due diligence to do this, then one will find that the only kind of faith He gives, as defined in His Word, is the one that **overcomes** the world (**John 16:33**; **1 John 2:13**).

Triumph Through Tenacity

This desire of His is verbalized by His Words in **Luke 18:1-8**; one that enables us to surmount our current life circumstances and soon, the horrible events that are about to unfold on our world sooner than we think, the kind of faith that meets His condition found, again, in **Revelation 3:10**:

> "**BECAUSE YOU** (addressing *each* one of us) *have **kept** the **Word*** of My endurance [My command to **persevere** by faith], I will ***keep you*** [*safe*] **from** the hour of trial (the tribulation period), that *hour*, which is about to come on *the whole* [inhabited] world, **to test those** who live on the earth."

If you are familiar with His message to all of the seven churches in the Book of Revelation, He continually tells them, "He *who overcomes*," gets His approval and a blessing from it. Having studied some 600 prophecies—over 400 fulfilled with unerring precision—I harbor no doubt that these dire events, which are approaching swifter than we anticipate.

An Urgent Summon

I believe that God implanted this message in my heart with urgency for these times, to share with the few who will pay attention to it with open minds and receptive spirits. Today's headlines merely foreshadow a grim reality of what's unfolding globally. People sense that "something wicked this way comes," yet remain perplexed, restless, and powerless, about something that it's not known or understood.

> Years ago, this conviction compelled me to take God and His Word seriously, and earnestly, for discerning these times now (**Matt. 16:3**; **Luke 21:36**)—not later, about what *I must* do, **before** His return.

Echoes of Unease

Such apprehensions were less palpable years ago (intensifying since 2020). Understandably, some, engrossed in their daily toil, overlook these omens. I aim to share this with those who will listen—for its eternal worth is immeasurable. I am concerned that God may hold me accountable if I withhold it from those He—and I—cherish and care about. I can only obey, trusting He will wield these words for those eager to learn and apply His Word in their daily lives.

A Fresh Revelation

All of these concepts and insights were novel to me as time went along, and perhaps to you as well. Nevertheless, in my 50 years of being a Christian, I've never encountered them in sermons, Christian texts, or church history. Instinctively, I sensed long ago, as I got familiar with His Word, that Christianity plumbed depths way deeper and beyond the superficial inputs coming from the religious establishments. Only upon completing and refining this work, am I coming to realize how profound they are. Thus, I am learning as I am writing, and hopefully, you, as you read. With that, let us continue.

Mixing Faith with Belief

Across my fifty years as a Christian, it took over thirty-five for me to realize that many—myself included initially, within and beyond churches—once more, confound belief (a form of hope) with **biblical faith**. The churches I attended preached faith that still echoes on Sundays today, making it as complicated as brain surgery. I suspect most pastors remain unaware of God's true faith, and its use in **Roman 12:3**—the one He bestows—not our self-crafted variants. This is the faith Jesus seeks in His probing question of **Luke 18:8**. I believe that He foresaw His Church's dire straits today, issuing this warning for our present times.

Paternal Counsel

Like an earthly father, cautioning his children to safeguard them within his shielding design, God imparts His knowledge through His Word, having foreseen its necessity for these last days. This eludes our grasp, for He transcends our temporal and spatial boundaries—past and future collapse into His eternal **now**. What He discerned 2,000 years ago (**Luke 18:8**) aligns with our current outlook. **Psalms 90:4** and **2 Peter 3:8** affirm:

> "Nevertheless, do not let this one **fact** escape your notice, beloved, that with the Lord **one day** is like a **thousand** years, and a **thousand** years is like one day."

I know, this is not easy to understand but it's a fact when we come to understand His Word, and the nature of eternity. Therefore, if we obey **all** of His commands, it gives Him free hand to fulfill any, and all of His promises in our lives that He has guaranteed to us, despite our shortcomings, and in that process, working all things together for good (**Rom. 8:28**), to complete His personalized plan of salvation for each one of us, from beginning to end (**Phil. 1:6**).

Faith That Unlocks Promises

Comprehending this divine concept of time, it defies ease of under-standing yet rings true when we engage His Word and the essence of what eternity is. Obeying His precepts activates and empowers every promise which is aligned with His plan for your life—despite our fal-tering—towards our good (**Romans 8:28**), culminating His redemp-tive purpose for each true child of His. Hence, Jesus lauded the faith of some—like the centurion (**Matthew 8:8**) or the woman grasping His hem—who believed steadfastly and reaped miracles (**Matthew 13:58; Mark 6:5**). Today, He seeks that kind of faith in us **if** we **trust** the truth of His promise in **Romans 12:3**.

Miracles in Our Days

We overlook that in His days, those around Him lacked the indwell-ing Holy Spirit and the privilege of having *His faith*. Since we pos-sess it today—what's our excuse for not wielding it? The sole dispar-ity, between then and now, is His *physical absence*, yet He remains with us via the Holy Spirit, if we *dare to believe* and *embrace* His personal promise to us in His Word of **John 14:26** and **16:13**.

What of Today?

Of course, the first question that pops up in our mind is, how can this happen today? Before I offer the answer to this question and hav-ing experienced myself dozens of miracles in my own life, let's review what He said in **John 14:12**:

> "I assure you *and* most solemnly say to you, **anyone** who **believes** in Me [in its *fullness*] will also **do** the things that **I do**; and he will do even *greater* things than these [in extent and outreach], *because* I am going to the Father."

Greater Works Await

I can already hear the retort:

> "Then He said, 'Doubtless you will quote Me this proverb:
> Physician, heal yourself! All the miracles we've heard You per-
> formed in Capernaum, do here in Your hometown too'" (**Luke
> 4:23**).

Though I'm not pointing fingers at anybody, the answer to this
is straightforward: **none of us** possesses the **full spectrum** of the
Holy Spirit's gifts as He did (**John 3:34; 1 Corinthians 12**). Yet,
any of us can witness and experience miracles in our lives through
mere belief in what He says in His Word. Over fifty years, I've seen
hundreds—small and great. He asserts that our **unbelief** alone is our
shortfall; if practice makes perfect, why not begin believing now? If
not now, when?

Empowered From Above

While many of us haven't attained absolute belief, Jesus endowed us
with all the required power for any situation present in our life. In
Luke 24:49, He affirms to **each** one of us:

> "Listen carefully: I am sending the **Promise of My Father** [the
> Holy Spirit] upon **you**; but you are to remain in the city [of
> Jerusalem] until you are clothed (*fully equipped*) with **power**
> from on high."

The world daily echoes that same taunt to Christians—
"Physician, heal yourself!" So why not demonstrate it today?
Tragically, the world does not know that many Christians fail to
manifest this to them because, to begin with, they are illiterate about
His Word and the promises within, and second, they, while professing to follow Him, they are living a life that is indistinguishably
from theirs. Yet one can attest—as I can—that **any life** is profoundly
transformed post-salvation **IF**, and it's a big if, conforms to His plan

by just obeying His instructions found in it. However, if one compromises their integrity or honesty, to avoid "offending" others, and neglecting righteousness in all things for all people, how can any of us behold any miracles?

This is what validates Jesus' power and promises in **Luke 24:49**, quoted above, and I am here to say to anyone that He has fulfilled that in my own life. Every **need** (**not** *my wants*) in my life has been fully met for the last 25 years according to His instructions in **Matt. 6:33**.

Abundance Through Christ

There is a reason why most Christians, including myself at the beginning of my walk with Him, were living a life of financial want and need, because we were following broken down and defective instructions from a pulpit, cassette, books, etc. So, how on earth could we even be able to *receive* all of His promises especially, that one found in **John 10:10**?

"I came that *they may have and enjoy life*, and have it in *abundance* [to the full, till it overflows]."

This promise fuels the devil's relentless assault to keep a lot of Christians joyless, despondent, and broke. Yet they remain ignorant of the authority Jesus bestowed to **all of us** in **Luke 10:19**:

> "Listen carefully: I have **given you** authority [that **you** now **possess**] to tread on serpents and scorpions, and [the *ability to exercise authority*] over **ALL** the *power of the enemy* (Satan); and **NOTHING** will [in any way] harm you."

Crucially, this authority is granted solely to **disciples** who embrace and exercise God's faith—not to mere believers. The distinction? A disciple, in faith, **trusts, relies, adheres**, and obeys Him. A believer merely accepts *hearsay* from religious men because they are unacquainted with the Word, and not knowing **who He is**, and *who* **they are** *in Him* (read **Eph. 2:6**; **Heb. 12:22**, **Eph. 4:7**; **2 Tim. 1:7**). But once the Holy Spirit unveils our spiritual eyes—when we surrender our will to His—we grasp that the devil's power to assail

Christians stems from our **own disobedience** to God's mandates for *not living* the way He commanded us to live (**Isaiah 59:1-2; 1 John 5:17**).

Discipleship Defined

How do we discern a disciple from a believer? Simple—He tells us in **John 8:31**:

> " So, Jesus was saying to the Jews who had believed Him, '**If** you **abide** in My Word [**continually obeying** My teachings and **living** in accordance with them, **then**] *you* **are** *truly My disciples.*"
>
> (See **John 13:35**, and the motive for obedience in **John 14:15, 14:21-23**).

The Devil's Leverage

Ignore all of His conditions for you to use His authority, and we're easy prey, stumbling into folly (**Romans 6:16-22**), **empowering** the devil to ravage our lives. So, the question is, would you prefer to live using **His** authority—or using your **own** for the benefit of your enemy to wreck your life, or even destroy you?

Read again **Luke 10:19**, "Listen carefully: I have given you **authority** that you **now possess** (*not* in the sweet by and by, or after death, but **NOW**)."

A Gradual Awakening

Rest assured; most Christians are in the *same boat*, just the same as I was in it myself, by *not* being aware about this authority, which *is available* to **all of us** when I first became a Christian. However, little by little over a long period of time and, as simple as this may sound to you, it just happened to me by my decision to **personally** read, rather than hear from others, His own Word, and *allowing* His Spirit to be sidetracked, instead of by faith, Him opening the scriptures to us (review **Luke 24:27**; and **24:45**), as <u>**promised**</u> in **John 14:26**, and **16:13**.

A Transformative Habit

I began reading the Bible cover-to-cover annually, then biannually, in *under* an hour daily. The transformations in my life and struggles were so profound, I'd do it now even if it took twelve hours a day.

An Unplanned Miracle

Did I orchestrate this? No—I had no inkling of what would transpire once I engaged His Word, yet the outcomes have been astounding. My counsel: pray before reading, beseech the Spirit to *unlock* and open your heart, and spiritual eyes, and ears. He's my witness: it unfolds organically, without my striving or effort—His Spirit wrought it all within me. In fifty years as a Christian, no sermon, talk, or study has presented, or broached this—*only God does it, not any church or religion*.

Word-Driven Change

This is my impetus for penning this message. I don't fault churches or pastors—I suspect they're as unaware about this as I once was. This dawned on me, only in the last twelve years, solely by immersing myself in, and letting His Word permeate my entire being.

Life in the Spirit

As mentioned, I have only come to experience this in my own life, over the last 12 years or so, as His Word began to soak in and infusing my inner man with His Word. This is the embodiment of what He tells us in **John 6:63**:

> "It is the *Spirit who gives life*; the flesh conveys *no benefit* [it is of no account]. The words I have spoken to you <u>**are spirit and life**</u> [providing eternal life]."

Only His living Word transformed me from **within** (**John 7:38**)—not vice versa, as my Bible teachers said and then me trying to do this on my own when I first became a convert. Again, I am not blaming churches or pastors because they might not know these things themselves. After all, they primarily teach out of their own intellectual and religious pool of knowledge and on what others have taught them in seminaries.

Why the Struggle?

Why is this simplicity of the gospel is so elusive to Christianity at large when it's freely offered to all His children? Again, **Hosea 4:6** explains it:

> "My people are *destroyed for* **lack** of **knowledge** [of My law, (our Bible) where I **reveal** My will]. Because you [the priestly nation (see **1 Peter 2:9**)] have **rejected** knowledge (of His Word), I will also **reject you** from being My priest. Since you have **forgotten** (*think*: how can anyone remember it without reading it?) **the law** (our Bible) of your God, I will also forget your children."

Disobedience's Cost

Our Lord provides a myriad Old Testament examples—obedience in Abraham, Isaac, Jacob, and King David, disobedience in Cain, Lot's wife, king Saul, and countless other kings in both kingdoms in Israel. Choosing the disobedience path and the *judgment* of **Hosea 4:6** not only exiles us from His **protection**, *provision*, and *blessing*, like what happened to the prodigal son in the parables, but also, **jeopardizes our inheritance**, as the slaves from Egypt forfeited theirs. **Isaiah 59:1-2** reveals why:

> "Behold, the Lord's hand is **not** so short that it cannot save, nor His ear so impaired that it cannot hear. But **your** *wickedness* (**not doing** His will in your life) has **separated you** (individually) from **your** God, and **your** sins (our offensive behavior towards Him through our **disobedience**, just like the slaves out

of Egypt) have **hidden** His face from **you**, so that He does **not hear** [you]."

A Just Consequence

Is God unjust? No! If a pilot spurns the manual for flying the plane he is operating and crashes, is the manufacturer Boeing to blame? As we can see, it's not that complicated, is it? So, if we **fail** to understand the implications of the two warning in the verse above, then, all things being equal, just how can any Christian make God *responsible* for his/her disobedience for failing to attain, and experience, any of His blessing and/or promises? There is a full range of reasons and issues for this outcome that is present in most of the lives of Christians today, some of which, we are about to discuss.

Rejecting the Warnings

If we spurn His admonitions, how can we fault God for unfulfilled promises? In **Isaiah 58**, He laments His longing for Israel's **obedience** to unleash His blessings, yet they—like too many Christians of today—rebuffed to *comply* with His Word. Small wonder, then, that they **failed**, like the church today, to live the abundant life of **John 10:10**, neither trusting nor wielding His God given faith, or the *authority we already have* of **Luke 10:19**.

Dismantling the Divide

Only we can remove that wall of unbelief, and our distrust of His promises in His Words, and by not depending on Him totally (**Psalms 5:11, 9:10**; **Romans 9:33**, and in **10:11**). We are the ones who erected this wall of separation between Him and us, and therefore, we are the ones who must remove this roadblock through our **obedience**.

Again, don't fret because this process is not like having Instant Oatmeal, but it's a sequence of *personal decisions* and the events that they **will** bring about, to your own benefit, that will be tailor-made to each one of us **IF**, we decide to *listen and obey* His instructions and commands clearly spelled out in His Word, just as when He *instructed* His saved people when they came out of Egypt.

A Gradual Unfolding

Be it a minor hiccup, or a monumental crisis, fret not—these transformations don't materialize magically. It's a bespoke odyssey of personal resolve and determination, distinct for each one of us. Yet, if we heed and obey His Word, we'll sidestep the fate of the Exodus wanderers—this is clearly illustrated and seen in the story of Exodus where a trip from Egypt (our station of life when we come to Jesus), to the Promised Land in Canaan, which shouldn't have taken no more than a few weeks, took 40 years. However, **only two**, who were not stubborn or rebellious **out** of **600,000+ men**, entered, and experienced the life He promised in the Promised Land which today, for us, is His promise found in **John 10:10**.

Many Called Few Chosen

However, reflect on this—out of 603,550 Jews, **only two** arrived into the Promised Land. This disproportionate ratio of God's people who answered the call of Moses to be saved from slavery, is what our Lord was referring as, "*many are called, but few chosen.*" For us, reaching *our Promised Land* is coming to experience the abundant life of **John 10:10** in **this life**, *not the next*.

In **Numbers 1:3**, God ordered to take a census of all the freed slaves who were twenty years old and up and the total number of all tribes came to all who were numbered were 603,550 (**Numb. 1:46**). Later, in **chapter 13**, Moses sent the 12 spies into Cannan to survey the land. So, we can readily see that 603,548 died in the vine without reaching God's *purpose* for them. Something to think about if we want the best He has to offer.

Prioritizing the Divine

There are many other directives, but in my estimation, the most important one for the Christian today, is the one found in **Matt. 6:33**:

> "**Above all else**, pursue (relentlessly chase, labor for) God's kingdom and His righteousness [His standard of integrity—His disposition and essence], and **all these things** (your well-being, health, finances, without exception) will be bestowed upon you too."

Let's be frank: what befalls to most worldly souls who turn to Christ? They *persist* in banking on the world and their own strength for their provision, does it not? I've walked that path—worn that shirt—but no more, thanks to Almighty God, as I substantiate this promise daily.

Chapter Two

Avoiding the Hosea 4:6 Judgement

Echoes of History

In the **Book of Hebrews** chapters **3** and **4** unravel why we let go the life of **John 10:10**, the potency of **Luke 24:49**, and the dominion of **Luke 10:19**. **Hebrews 3:18-19** reveals this to His Church today:

> "And to whom did He swear [an oath] that they **would not enter** His rest, if not to those who defied [*unwilling* to *follow* His Word]? Thus, we see **they** (and Christians today) could *not enter* [His rest—the promised land] due to **unbelief and refusal** to trust God."

His words cut with clarity, don't they? Before plunging deeper, let's anchor His intent and purpose in *authoring* the Old Testament—a design sculpted for us today, to illuminate lessons veiled (**Proverbs 25:2**) from Genesis to Malachi, tailored for His offspring.

Scripture's Purpose

Romans 15:4 attests:

> "For whatever *was written* in earlier times (that is the O.T.), it was written for *our instruction*, so that through endurance and

the encouragement **of the <u>Scriptures</u>**, we might have ***<u>patience</u>*** [endurance] *and* overflow with ***<u>confidence</u>*** in His ***<u>promises</u>***."

He reinforces this Old Testament aim in **1 Corinthians 10:6**:

"Now these things [the warnings and admonitions] took place as **<u>examples for us</u>**, so that **<u>we</u>** would **<u>not</u>** crave evil things as they did."

He pinpoints here, what conducts in our life are ***offensive*** to Him—deeds we must eschew today ***if we seek* <u>communion</u> *with Him*, 24/7** if we desire it. For those who crave this, one must have a knowledge the entire New Testament which furnishes us His ***rules and conditions*** to forge a life that is unoffensive to Him.

The Heart of This Discourse

Before advancing further, one must grasp the core of this discourse, and keep it in focus: it's a solemn warning about losing our inheritance in Him. It also analyzes and breaks down why countless Christian lives—including mine post-salvation—floundered in disarray. By God's mercy, I ceased ***obstructing*** His blueprint and plan for me, and He guided me to jettison the worldly junk and the religious debris. I swerved from my errant course, by merely ***removing*** my ignorance about His Word.

A Recurring Truth

I've quoted it often, and it bears repeating, for this verse **<u>unveils why</u>** our Christian existence languishes in the here and now, plus a real danger of being disinherited by being absent of a full-time fellowship with Him. This is the **<u>result</u>** of ignoring His warning in **Hosea 4:6**:

"My people are destroyed (by our enemy, and His) for **<u>lack</u>** of **<u>knowledge</u>** [of My law (our Bible), where I **<u>reveal My will</u>**]. Because **<u>you</u>** [the priestly nation (see **1 Peter 2:9**)] have **<u>rejected</u>**

knowledge (of His Word), I will also reject **you** from being **My priest**."

(see what His *goal is* in **Exodus 19:6**, and what it **is** today for us, and the *true nature* and *substance* for today's Christian, in **1 Peter 2:9**).

A Lasting Reminder

It may bother you, but God wants **Hosea 4:6** to *shape*, *influence*, and give *character* to your **heart and mind**, so that you can be a priest before Him for the rest of your eternity. This transformation will become the tool and the yardstick that will teach you to discern the difference, between establishing biblical truth, or error.

Dual Witness to Truth

As you may have noticed, I invariably cite **two or more Scriptures** to bolster His message and establish His truth, per His mandate for **verifying** a truth. **Deuteronomy 19:15**, **Matthew 18:16**, and **2 Corinthians 13:1** stipulate:

> "This is the third time that I am visiting you. **Every truth** [fact] shall be **sustained and confirmed** by the testimony of two or three witnesses."

(See also **1 Timothy 5:19**; **Hebrews 10:28**.)

Thus, **any** biblical matter establishing a dogma, doctrine, and/ or creed, demands and **must** have multiple verses echoing the same principle and premise.

Doctrinal Pitfalls

This approach—validating God's truth and logic of His promises and salvation plan—necessitates dual scriptural support, particularly to distinguish the nature of salvation. It's crucial to thwart fallacious doctrines rooted in solitary verses, as every spurious Christian sect and cults attests.

This shields God's children from **deception** by religions or factions (**2 Corinthians 11:3**; **Ephesians 4:14**). Consider the Mormons: they assert that the "I have other sheep" (**John 10:16**) verse, denotes that their church is the "true church," yet not a **single secondary verse** substantiates this—He was speaking about the gentiles that later were reached by Paul's ministry.

Yet, this absurd, unsubstantiated notion nearly lured me, as a naive new convert, to join this cult. Seventh-day Adventists peg their doctrines to the Sabbath, but Colossians **2:16-18** easily debunks these beliefs:

> "Therefore let **no one judge** you in regard to food and drink or in regard to [the observance of] a festival or a new moon or a **Sabbath day**. Such things are only *a shadow* of what is to come, *and* they have **only symbolic value**; but the substance [the **reality** of what is foreshadowed] belongs to Christ."
>
> But even better, read the whole **chapter 2** of this book that blows away just about every exclusive doctrines of the so-called "Christian religions."

This rule extends to debunk the Catholic confessional booth, Jehovah's Witnesses rejecting Christ's Divinity, Baptists with their baptismal beliefs, and beyond. **Any** Bible-savvy Christian can dismantle these religious manmade fallacies to the dust where they belong.

Salvation vs. The Kingdom

This egregious flaw—lacking corroborative secondary Scriptures to Bible grounded doctrines—permeates denominations, cults, and sects, which are deep and enduring. However, a disciple who is being tutored by His Spirit can immediately identify these distortions as blatantly erroneous and misleading; but what about those which are *subtler* snares to mislead you into a religion, rather than the truth?

A Personal Deception

As an example of such cunning and insidious deceptions, found in every religion seeking for more paying members, permit me to recount my own deception, while trying to develop my own spiritual house foundation into the Christian faith, two young Mormon missionaries had me convinced that they were the "only true church" on that solitary verse in **John 10:16**, above. Only common sense would reveal to anyone that God was **NOT** twiddling His thumbs until 1844 to "restore the 'true' church" after millions of people went to hell while He waited for Joseph Smith. The idea of it is totally ridiculous, if not outright irrational and bizarre! Yet, 15 million or more people don't think it is.

Another of the many pervasive errors being propagated across the religious establishment is conflating salvation with an inherent "right" to **enter** God's Kingdom, presuming this divine realm is synonymous with redemption itself. This sly supposition insinuates that such privilege is intrinsic to our salvation. Yet, as we'll explore, **it is not**—allow me to dismantle this thoughtless idea here.

In the gospels, our Lord likens the Kingdom to objects of **immense _value and worth_** in several passages. Take just one in **Matthew 13:44**:

> "The kingdom of heaven is like a [very precious] treasure hidden in a field, which a man found and hid again; then in his joy he goes and **sells all he has and buys** that field [securing the treasure for himself]."

A Flawed Substitution

Here's the simple test: if salvation equates to the **_same as the Kingdom_**, let's substitute in the same verse the word "salvation," for "kingdom":

> "Salvation is like a [very precious] treasure hidden in a field, which a man found and hid again; then in his joy he goes and **sells all he has and buys** that field [**_securing_** salvation for himself]."

Now, a glaring question emerge: What did I, or anyone else, had to sell to procure our salvation? What possession of mine could be worth enough to purchase the universe's paramount treasure—our Lord's sacrifice on the cross?

Surely, seeing this disparity, one would have to accept that there's no correlation between these two concepts. However, keep this in the back of your mind because **there is a reason** <u>why</u> He used these parables to make an important point to unmask all of the religious deceptiveness seen today.

As we will see later, by the end of this writing, you will perceive what our Lord was trying to tell His disciples, and each one of us, something important because the Kingdom's value demands its pursuit once we **understand** how valuable it is, and what **one must do** to **inherit it**—because **it's not free**.

Distinct Eternal Stakes

This distinction—that salvation alone doesn't grant Kingdom entry—is pivotal, determining **where**, not merely **how**, one will spend eternity post-rapture, or our death. I'll substantiate biblically that the Kingdom of God bears **no tie** whatsoever, to our freely bestowed salvation. This theme permeates all four gospels.

A cursory study of His Word—not what you hear from pastors, preachers, or teachers schooled in human wisdom by religious institutions, where all of their "spiritual knowledge" is gleaned from seminaries, books, or fallible sources—reveal their lackluster results in any average neighborhood church. Such spiritual inaccuracies, rife with theological discord, **cannot** stem from His Spirit, or His Word.

The proof? If they were speaking, and were led by His Spirit, there would be **NO divisions** whatsoever among them (**Hebrews 13:8; Philippians 1:27; Ephesians 4:4**), and thousands of other discordant religions, denominations, and cults wouldn't proliferate, preaching notions alien to His Word.

Spirit Superiority Over a Religious System

This is easy to deduce because, as we keep unpacking God's Word, it will be proved that He **never** sanctioned religious institutions to instruct His New Testament saints apart from His Spirit. He reserved that privilege only for Old Testament Jews via the Aaronic Priesthood and Levitical order. To claim otherwise for the Church, raises a glaring query: if the system of today that mirrors that Jewish religious structure, and they do today, **why endow us** then with His indwelling Spirit to teach us, as **affirmed** in **John 14:26, 15:26,** and **16:13**?

Clearly, Jesus labored to distinguish the Law's spirit from its stone-etched letter—beloved by the Pharisees then, and those of today—It's equally obvious then that the purpose of His Spirit is to do the *same thing* for us today, as that of what Jesus **did** in the flesh, with His own disciples back then! I will prove this intention and objective of His, beyond a reasonable doubt as you will see throughout this whole narrative.

Linguistic Clarity

Consider this religious fallacy—equating the Kingdom with salvation—via the Greek terms used. "**Salvation**" (**Luke 19:9**, [*sōtēria*]) denotes:

[**deliverance** from enemies' harassment (Satan for us); *preservation*, *safety* [from]; *salvation*]"

Contrast this definition, with "Kingdom of God" (**Matthew 3:2**):

Kingdom of *(basileia)* denotes:

[*royal power*, *kingship*; *dominion*; *rule*].

God *(ouranos)* denoting:

[*the vaulted sky's expanse (heaven) and all that's visible therein*].

No genius required here—these two terms are incongruent with each other. Note this disparity because the passage in **Revelation 22:12-15** will unveil how understanding this obvious difference, dictates our eternal **place** and **rank** in the kingdom to come. I ***cannot overemphasize*** the gravity of knowing this.

Salvation's Scope

In what context does His Word declare us saved, and from what? **Ephesians 2:4-5** (Amplified in the Greek) elucidates:

> "But God, being [so very] rich in mercy, because of His great and wonderful love with which He loved us, even when we were [spiritually] dead and separated from Him because of our sins, He made us [spiritually] **alive** (as compared to *dead* when we are born) together **with** Christ (for by His grace—His undeserved favor and mercy—you have been **saved FROM** God's **judgment** (wrath))."

We can find the **second witness** to this truth in **Romans 5:9**, among many others:

> "Therefore, since we have now been justified [declared *free* of the *guilt* of sin] by His blood, [how much more certain is it that] we will be *saved* **FROM** the **wrath** of God **through** Him."

Beyond Salvation Lies the Act of Being Chosen

Unless we come to understand that **being saved does not mean being chosen**, then this *ignorance will erect a wall* that prevents one from getting there. Satan has been extremely successful in this area of keeping the sheep blind to this fact through the religion's knack of implying things that are not written, defined, or implied in God's Word.

In **Nehemiah 9:7**, God say that He chose Abraham using the Hebrew word (*bāḥar*), which simply means—"*to be chosen, selected*." Now, in **Matt. 22:14**, our Lord used the Greek word (*eklektos*) when He said, "many are called but few *chosen*," which means—*chosen, choice, select*, i.e., the *best of its kind or class, excellence*, **preeminent**. Both, the Hebrew, with a slight change (*bāḥîr*, rather than "*bāḥar,*"), is interchangeable with the word "*elect.*" I don't have to labor the point that when our Lord said, "many are called," using the Greek word (*klētos*), for "*called,*" is referring to all of those **called to salvation**, not for **election**. Why? It's as simple as the fact that one has to first **accept** the call for our own selves and then **elect** and **choose** *to fulfill the requirements* of that office.

This is what He says in **1 Cor. 12:28-30**:

> "So, God has appointed ([*tithēmi*] meaning to **establish**, **ordain**, but not necessarily for someone to **accept** it) *and* placed in the church [for His own use]: first apostles [chosen by Christ], second prophets [those who foretell the future, those who speak a new message from God to the people], third teachers, then those who work miracles, then those with the gifts of healings, the helpers, the administrators, and speakers in *various* kinds of [unknown] tongues. Are **all** apostles? Are **all** prophets? Are **all** teachers? Are **all** workers of miracles? Do **all** have gifts of healing? Do **all** speak with tongues? Do **all** interpret?"

It's obvious that the answer is **NO**! And by the same token, not **all** of those called to salvation are going to *be chosen*, or be *part of the elect*, **UNLESS** one chooses to commit to His calling.

As far as I am concerned, this is not rocket science nor debatable in terms of plain common sense. So, I will leave that to you and God to decide what He means with His Words.

By Grace, Not Anything We Do

Therefore, let's now move forward by establishing what is the **general basis** for our salvation:

> "**Is by *grace*** [God's remarkable compassion and favor for, *it is He*, who **draws** you to Christ (see John 6:37; 44; and 65)] that you have been *saved* [actually *delivered* **FROM** *judgment* (from God's *wrath*, as discussed above) and given eternal life] *through faith* (and not by *what* you *do*, but by *what* you *practice* and *do* because of *Whom* you *believe*). And this [salvation]

is not of yourselves [not through your own effort], but it is the [undeserved, gracious] **gift** of God" (**Eph. 2:8**).

This clarifies that salvation hinges not on what we do, think, or believe, or any other mental construct (that shapes habits), but on **only** on **what we're spared** from. Yet, if His Spirit reigns in us, our lives **will reflect His work** within by, and **through**, our **obedience** to His Word—but of course, only **IF** we know what His Word says.

Imitating the Divine

We're called to **mirror** Him (review **James 1:23**), as **Ephesians 5:1** urges:

> "Therefore, become *imitators* of God [*copy* Him and *follow* His example], as well-beloved children [imitate their father]" (also read **1 Cor. 11:1**, and **4:16**)."

And how can we do this? Recall **Genesis 1**? "And God said"—and His Spirit brought to pass. **Hebrews 11:3** explains:

> "We understand that the worlds (universe, ages) were framed and created [formed, put in order, and equipped for their intended purpose] **by the Word of God**, so that **what is seen** *was* **not mad**e out of things which are **visible**."

Thus, **voicing** His promises from a heart-rooted belief—not intellect—prompts God to honor our prayers and materialize them by His Spirit (**Romans 8:26**; **Zech. 4:6**). This *demands* practice **UNTIL** it become our ethos (**1 Samuel 16:7**; **Proverbs 21:2**; **Matthew 15:11**, and verse **18**).

The Word As Our Authority

Why belabor this? To embolden us to affirm His Word as the sole, ultimate arbiter of truth—not men's opinions, doctrines, or religious conjectures coming from churches and religions everywhere. I pray you'll see that these aren't "my ideas" but His, as etched in Scripture. Were they mine, they'd be futile. Without this internal assent, unchecked religious claims spawn countless "Christian" sects. I don't seek agreement, but urge you to scrutinize this biblically, emulating the Bereans who:

> "Were more noble and **open-minded** than those in Thessalonica, so they *received* the message with great eagerness, **examining the Scriptures** daily to see if these things were so" (**Acts 17:11**).

Faith Beyond the Mind

Seeking Spirit's Confirmation

Yet beyond this, if we genuinely *seek* His Spirit to *affirm* these truths, letting them take root in our hearts—not merely in our intellect—this act of faith demands we embrace them in our spirit, wielding His faith we have **already received** from **Romans 12:3**. Only then can we prove to ourselves, irrefutably, that He means precisely what His Word declares. It's solely on this foundation—His promises in **John 14:26** and in **16:13**—that His Spirit unveils these realities personally, illuminating His precepts and redemptive plan. This spurs us to take them earnestly, meditate upon them, and act on them daily.

With that prelude, let God's Word now shepherd us into discerning the difference between hope and that of an authentic faith.

Defining Faith's Essence

It's no fluke then that God gifted us its definition in **Hebrews 11:1-2**:

> "Now faith is the *assurance* (title deed, confirmation) of things hoped for (divinely **guaranteed**), and the evidence of things not seen [the *conviction* of their reality—faith comprehends **as fact**, what **cannot** be experienced by the **physical senses**]. For by this [*quality* of] faith the **men of old** gained [divine] *approval*."

He pairs this with the **method** in **Romans 10:17**:

"So, faith _**comes**_ from _**hearing**_ [what is told], and what is heard _**comes**_ by the **message** (in our Bibles) _**concerning**_ Christ."

In human terms, it's crystal clear: **Hebrews 11** frames faith as _**assurance**_ and _**evidence**_; **Romans 10:17** reveals that it flows from hearing Christ's message. It's that simple, isn't it?

It's no different than buying a car, I trust its warranty without fretting future repairs. If I trust a manufacturer, why waver with the guarantee from the universe's Creator? Yet we do just that, muddling hope—a mere wish—with our own human faith, as if it was firm conviction. This isn't sloppy reasoning; it's the fallout of _**leaning**_ on human effort, or flimsy church doctrines over that of God's Spirit. Why, then, would I do that, and curse myself, as **Jeremiah 17:5** warns by trusting on man, by heeding men over His Spirit? That's spiritual self-induced sabotage!

Christ's Perfect Example

Although Jesus didn't need baptism—He was sinless (**John 8:48**), nor did He lose His fellowship with the Father in Eden—but He did it anyway "to fulfill all righteousness" (**Matthew 3:15**), modeling for the faith we're gifted with, **not** one that we can "seek, grow it, or produce it ourselves—**Romans 12:3** says God apportions it to us and **is perfect** as is (**James 1:17**).

The truth is that our Lord lived for 33 years as a _**perfect**_, _**real human being**_, fulfilling the Law of Moses because no human being could do it, and then being an example for us (see **Romans 8:29**; **1 Corinthians 15:20-23**; **Colossians 1:18**; **Hebrews 1:6**, and others)—but He allowed Himself to be baptized "to fulfill" an **equality** between Him being Divine, and us in our humanity (**Matthew 3:15**; and **12:47-49-50**). This act of baptism was Jesus' way of identifying Himself with sinners whose sins He would ultimately bear, and to whom His righteousness would be imparted to show **why our faith must come from Him**, because it **must be perfect** (**Romans 12:3**;

James 1:17). This is our only way to be **able** to *follow in His footsteps*. Before shrinking from this, consider **Ephesians 2:6**:

"And [He] **raised us** up together [(with Jesus) when we believed] and **made us sit together** [**with Him**] in the heavenly places [**because we are**] in Christ Jesus."

Fulfilling Righteousness

His baptismal words in **Matthew 3:15** unpack this:

"But Jesus said to him, 'Let it be so now; for this is the way **we must fulfill all righteousness** before God (His righteousness, not ours, because He never lost it in the Garden). So, John permitted it [and baptized him].'"

He underwent baptism to fulfill **Isaiah 51:7**, embedding it in our lives:

"Listen to Me, you **who know righteousness** (right standing with God), the people in **whose heart is My law** and **instruction**; do not fear the reproach and taunting of man, nor be distressed at their reviling."

(This is a reality present **only**, to those **knowing** His Word as taught **through** His Spirit and not by us, a church, denomination, or a religion).

That is the implication in His statement to John the Baptist in **Matthew 3:15**, above, and the reason why we are given a **Romans 12:3** faith that is **outside** of ourselves, given to **each** of His born-again children who have **believed** (the gospel) and **trusted** (in faith) in His Son.

Unlearning Religious Ruts

Early on, I swallowed the notion that I was the one who had to "look, find, and grow" my faith via my church teachings, and bringing it about by my own human efforts. Why hunt for something that's already yours? I leaned on pastors, books, and tapes to unravel

Scripture, ingesting opinions—mine and theirs—rather than letting the Spirit instruct.

At first, as a new Christian, I believed and accepted these religious teachings without thinking, because they said that this teaching "came" from the "Word of God"—well, His Word proves them wrong.

Since the third century, monasteries and seminaries have bred biblical illiteracy, not revelation. **Isaiah 54:13, Ezek. 34:20-24, Jerem. 31:33-34, Matt. 23:8, John 6:45,** and **John 14:26** and in **16:13**, pledge *direct*, <u>**divine teaching**</u>. These <u>**seven**</u> scripture passages above, a significant number by Bible standards, attest to this truth, and the importance of it—yet we've erected systems echoing **Genesis 3:1-7**—Satan twisting God's Word to Eve, who received it <u>**secondhand**</u> from Adam. Misspoken words from the pulpits and then, I had to unlearn all of it. History bares this flaw, and I don't deem it's done with malice—just Eve-like zeal gone awry. Trust me, this <u>**isn't**</u> anti-church at all—it's rather ***pro-truth***. God's Word, <u>**un-mediated**</u> by men, equips us to live boldly. That's the kind of faith that's **worth** chasing after it.

Spirit Over Stewards

God entrusted Old Testament oracles to the Aaronic priesthood and no doubt, He knew that they would fail, and anticipating their stumble, He did it anyway. Why? It's easy to figure it out, He was showing, *for our benefit today*, the very **reason <u>why</u> He <u>chose His Spirit over man</u>**—until Jesus, the "One Shepherd" (**Jeremiah 34:20-23**) came, who realigned the divine blueprint of His salvation. Today, we're not to strain faith, like gnats, through pulpits. Churches aid fellowship and worship (**Ephesians 4:11**), but the Spirit teaching is supreme. Clinging to men courts for explanations, is to invite Eve's deception.

Since He is the One *giving* His faith to us, **He**, not us, is the One that we are to collaborate with, ***despite*** ourselves with our shortcomings, and because it **does not** come from the flesh, or from our own flawed efforts, imaginations, or our inconsistent human spirit (read **James 1:6**). It is only when our spirit is **connected**, **integrated**, and **united**, with His Holy Spirit, just like our Lord was, is when we are **empowered** to walk in His footsteps.

Faith, Not Fabrication

Before pressing on, grasp why we conflate belief with faith—looking beyond the religious distortion that assumes that our belief mimics God's faith—it doesn't make it so, it remains useless because it's human (**John 6:63**), and the reason **why** He bestows it to us (**Romans 12:3**). He is the only One who can work with, and through it, despite our flaws, untainted by fleshly effort or a fickle human spirit (**James 1:6**). Only when our spirit aligns with His—mirroring our Lord's—does it thrive.

Why waste His faith for ours when we can use His? As stated above, if it's perfect already (**James 1:17**), how on earth could we then try and "make it better," as my churches taught me? It's irrational! If I possess it, why seek churches for it? I never pondered this until He exposed me to its futility—man's works are vain (**Jeremiah 17:5**; **John 6:63**; **1 Corinthians 1:20**). Yet every church I attended peddled this spiritual nonsense. As a novice believer, I injected this spiritual "hopium," and dubbed it as being "Christian truth," unthinkingly.

A Legacy of Illiteracy

Believe it or not, this denominational pedagogy—born in third-century monasteries, refined in post-Reformation seminaries—has spawned rampant biblical illiteracy across Christendom. Worse, its purveyors don't suspect their divergence from God's intent, as **Isaiah 54:13**, **John 14:26**, and **16:13** attest, clashes with this overconfident system. This ignorance wreaks havoc, prying open doors to myriad spiritual errors within every church edifice. Analyze it: it's a modernized **Genesis 3:1**:

> "Now the serpent was more crafty (subtle, *skilled in deceit*) than any living creature of the field which the Lord **God** had

made. And the serpent (Satan) said to the woman, 'can it **really be** *that* God **has said** (whatever is in His Word today), 'You shall not eat from *any tree* of the garden'?"

Satan's Subtle Twist

Missed the devil's sleigh? He misquotes God's Word, skewing its context—"not eat from **any** tree"—when God told Adam alone (**Genesis 2:15**), pre-Eve (**Genesis 2:21**). Eve heard it secondhand via Adam's "pulpit" (like us from men and religion today), and didn't catch God's actual decree said. Had she heard it directly from Him, she'd have retorted:

"No, what He said is that we can eat from *all* of them, **except** this one."

Our lack of knowledge mirrors hers and confirms what our Lord said in **Matt. 15:14**:

"Leave them alone; they are *blind guides* [leading *blind followers*]. If a blind man leads a blind man, both will fall into a pit."

Seeing the religious landscape of today, truer words have never been spoken.

The Peril of Secondhand Faith

Hearsay vs. Direct Revelation

Thus, I must underscore that, without firsthand knowledge of God's Word, you *cannot* distinguish between the Spirit's direct soft voice, and those from religious men's filtered echoes—prevalent in today's church settings. In any court of law, such secondhand testimony wouldn't stand; it's mere hearsay from a third party. If the Old Testament's writings is for instructing and admonishing us, what *les-*

son emerged from God entrusting men in the O.T.?—the Priesthood and Levitical system that crucified our Lord—the very same people who were entrusted to steward His oracles.

The answer is also found in an analysis of what happened to Moses' ministry and its ultimate outcome, as illustrated by the Pharisees and Sadducees when our Lord Jesus came to minister to His people. Just as in the Garden of Eden, He knew that if He again placed men in charge of teaching the saints of His New Testament Church, they would fail miserably again! And that has been the case, with the same outcome **for us** today, when this current fiasco was engendered back in the third century, and whatever good resulted from it, came through God's Grace. However, only disciples can discern this current spiritual state of affairs in the church today.

The Spirit Over That of Men

Why did He opt for His Spirit over human proxies? Simple: He harbors a loftier purpose for those who **choose** to *trust and rely* on Him alone. **Ezekiel 34:20-24** unveils His premeditated remedy:

> "Therefore, thus says the Lord God to them, 'Behold, **I Myself** (not your pastor or religion) will judge between the [well-fed] fat sheep and the lean sheep. Because you push with side and shoulder, and gore with your horns all those that have become weak and sick until you have scattered them away, therefore, **I will rescue** My flock (from who? Read verses **1-8**), and they shall no longer be prey; and I will judge between one sheep [ungodly] and another [godly]. Then I will appoint over them **ONE** shepherd and **He** (again, *not* your pastor or religion) **will feed** them, [a ruler like] My servant David; **He will feed** them (**ibid.**) and be their Shepherd (**ibid.**). And I, the Lord, will be their God, and My servant David will be a prince among them; I the Lord have spoken'."

This Levitical system's failure was duplicated by the first man-made Christian religion we know as Catholicism and mirrors the Jews' and Eve's destiny—secondhand spiritual scraps, still influenced and swayed by Eden's serpent. Now, for us, this knowledge is a double-edged sword: one edge is coming to know and understanding it, and the other is to remain oblivious to it—both inescapable, as **chapters 1-3** in **Hebrews** cautions.

It's no wonder then that God singled out the ***Corinthian and Galatian churches*** to chastise—for practicing religion, not faith—among the New Testament congregations. This is pointed out in **1 Corinthians 3:1-2**:

> "However, brothers and sisters, I could ***not*** talk to you **as** to **spiritual** people, but [only] as to ***worldly*** people, ***mere infants*** [in the **new life**] in Christ! I fed you with milk, ***not*** solid food; for you were not yet able *to receive* it. Even ***now***, you are **still not ready**."

And in **Galatians 1:7**:

> "Some [people masquerading as teachers] who are disturbing and confusing you [with a misleading, counterfeit teaching] and want to **distort** the gospel of Christ [twisting it into ***something*** which it absolutely **is not**]."

The Risk of Humans Teaching the Saints

This peril stalks any churchgoer opting for man's voice superseding that of the Spirit's, **defying** our Lord's directive in **John 14:26, 15:26**, and in **16:13**. This isn't a ban on church attendance should you choose to— join if you wish, but avoid personality cults, like that one of Joseph Smith, as the prime example—churches are for fellowship and worship, edified by Spirit-led, Bible-savvy pastors (**Ephesians 4:11**). I'm not "anti-church," but biblically, they're not sanctioned to disciple or teach—that's the Spirit's domain. Nothing's wrong being a member of any denomination, but ***not at the cost*** of God's tailored instructional model.

Satan's Subtle Mastery

The devil thrives at warping Scripture, deftly twisting truth to beguile church workers and pew-sitters alike. With six millennia experience of cunning and deception, he preys on the **unspiritual** through their lack of knowledge (**Hosea 4:6**)—and those in **Romans 7:14, 1 Corinthians 3:3, Colossians 2:18, James 3:15,** and **Jude 1:19.**

Five witness verses amplify this danger: ignorance leaves believers exposed in any pew, primed for deception like Eve. This has birthed hundreds of sects, denominations, and cults, defying **1 Corinthians 3:3-9**'s unity plea, echoed in **Ephesians 4:4**:

> "There is [**only**] **one** body [of believers] and **one** Spirit—just as you were called to **one** hope when **called** [to salvation]."
>
> Note: this calling is limited to salvation and grants **no** automatic Kingdom entry (**Revelation 22:15**), explaining "many are called, few chosen" (**Matthew 22:14; Mark 11:22; Romans 11:7**).

Satan Divides, God Unites

Why is this important for the Body? To begin with, He tells us this in **John 17:20-21**:

> "I do not pray for these alone [it is **not for their sake only** that I make this request], but also for [**all**] those who [will ever] believe *and* trust in Me through their message, that **they all may be one**; just as You, Father, are in Me and I in You, that they also may be **one in Us**, so that the world may believe [without any doubt] that You sent Me."

Ephesians 4:13 echoes the same purpose:

> "Until we all reach *oneness* in the faith and in the *knowledge* of the Son of God, [growing *spiritually*] to become a *mature believer*, reaching to the **measure** of the fullness of Christ [**manifesting** His spiritual completeness and exercising **our** spiritual gifts in **unity**]."

Who foments today's Christian schisms? Satan, peddling the lie that pulpits are His spokesmen and with impunity, they think that they can **usurp** the Ministry of God's Spirit—erecting a religious Babel over nineteen centuries, each chanting their own creed and their own version of "Jesus" made in their own particular religious image. If this escapes you, even a little, this here will snap you back into place when **2 Corinthians 4:3-4** nails it:

"But even if our [salvation] gospel is [in some sense] *hidden* [behind a *veil*], it is hidden [only] to those who are perishing (the lost nonbelievers, but for the Christians, is their *unbelief* in God's *Word* and *promises* made to every **disciple** of Christ); among them the god of this world [Satan] has blinded the *minds* of the unbelieving (and Christian church zealots) to *prevent* them from *seeing* the illuminating light of the gospel of the glory of Christ, who is the image of God."

The Veil of Tradition

This "veil" is Satan's secular ethos, duping not just the lost, but Christians as well, presenting modern churchianity as being equal with Christ's true Church. Sectarian dogma and traditions stifle new converts from day one, halting growth. Fellowship can aid, but only under Spirit-led pastors fostering a Christ-focused environment— rare, not routine. For infant believers craving intimacy with their Savior, this step does matter but the average pastor is clueless how to make a new convert grow spiritually. It's grim, but our mighty God prevails, as He did for me, per **1 Samuel 16:7**:

> "But the Lord said to Samuel, 'Do not look at his appearance or at the height of his stature, because I have rejected him. For the Lord sees **not** as man sees; for man looks [a]at the outward appearance, but the Lord looks at the **heart**'."

God's Unfailing Plan

God knows His own from eternity's dawn (**Ephesians 1:4; John 10:3**), guiding them to intimacy with Him (**Philippians 3:12; Titus**

2:14; **1 Peter 2:9**; **2 Peter 1:3**). I don't peg all church workers as malevolent; it's just that their teachings are steeped in human wisdom and tradition via skeptical professors in seminaries, which often lacks Spirit guidance. This flaw fuels a carousel—souls hop from being one day Catholic to Jehovah Witness, Protestant or Mormon the next—chasing ear-tickling doctrines (**2 Timothy 4:3**), over those of God's life, as modeled by Christ. They are willing to let others do the work that He asks **from us** as **Philippians 2:12** counters:

> "So then, my dear ones, just as you have always *obeyed* [my instructions with enthusiasm], not only in my presence, but now much more in my absence, *__continue__* to *__work out__* **your (own) salvation** [that is, cultivate it, bring it to *full effect*, actively *__pursue spiritual maturity__*] with awe-inspired fear and trembling [using serious caution and critical *__self-evaluation__* to avoid anything that might *offend* God or *discredits* the name of Christ]" (also in **2 Cor. 10:15**).

God tasks us with **obeying His instructions**, not those from of **any** denomination or religion.

The Ultimate Teacher

Imagine Einstein as your physics professor—why settle for some Joe Blow? Pastors should assist, but *only after* the Master trains them—Christ—via the Spirit. I brook no compromise. As a Spirit-taught believer, I certainly can discern those disciples He sends my way when I need to learn something new, or an assist for my personal growth, trusting in the **Deuteronomy 10:17**'s God:

> "The God of gods and the Lord of lords, the **great**, the **mighty**, the **formidable** God who does not show partiality nor take a bribe."

This unlocks growth resources. But, if on insists in doing it **his, or her own way**—like in Israel's wilderness rut—cages us, stalling progress. The risk? Missing the Spirit's ministry and God's resources and **potentially**, loss of an **eternal stake** in the inheritance of God's Kingdom, as **Luke 12:47-48** warns:

> "And that servant (that's us Christians) who **knew** his Master's **will**, (by knowing His Word) and yet did **_not_** get ready (**obedient** to it), or **act** in *accord with His will*, will be beaten (at the judgment seat of Christ, **1 Cor. 3:13**) with many lashes [of the whip], but the one who did not know it (not caring to know His Word) and did things worthy of a beating, will receive only a few [lashes]. For from **_everyone_** to whom much has been given, much will be **_required_**; and to whom they entrusted much, of him they will ask all the more."

Chapter Three

Craving for the Word

Milk for the Newborn

Let us begin with the premise that having God's resources guarantees our entire spiritual growth from beginning to end, are there any limits? No! Thus, should any believer want to advance to be a disciple and *truly begin to grow spiritually*, **1 Peter 2:2** has what it takes to do this:

> "like newborn babies [you *should*] long for the **pure** *milk* of the Word, so that *by it*, you may be nurtured *and* **grow** in *respect* to [our] *salvation* [*its ultimate fulfillment*]."

But for those who might be spiritually lethargic, **Hebrews 5:11-13** stings:

> "Concerning this (regarding Christ's Priesthood's **outcome** in *each one* of us, and its implications regarding our personal walk with Him) we have much to say, and it is hard to explain, since you have become *dull and sluggish* in [your spiritual] hearing *and* disinclined to **listen**. For though by this time, you **ought** to be teachers [because of the time you have had to learn these truths], you actually need someone to teach you *again the* **elementary principles** of God's Word [from the beginning], and you have come to be *continually* (as in a church environment) in **need** of milk, *not* solid food. For **everyone** who lives on milk

is [doctrinally *inexperienced* and] **unskilled** in the Word of righteousness (that is, primarily knowing **Your Bible** as **taught** by men, not **BY** His Spirit), since he is a **spiritual infant**."

Pressing Toward Maturity

And in the following chapter of **Hebrews 6:1-3**, presses further:

> "Therefore, let us get **past the elementary stage** in the teachings about the Christ, *advancing* on to *maturity* and perfection and spiritual completeness, [doing this] **without** laying **again** a foundation from dead works and of faith toward God, of teaching about washings (ritual purifications), the laying on of hands, the resurrection of the dead, and eternal judgment. [These are all important matters in which **you** should have been **proficient** long ago]. And we *will do* this [that is, proceed to maturity], if God permits."

As a fledgling, new believer, these verses baffled me. I saw no tangible maturity in myself—His promises flickered inconsistently in my life, nor could I claim the triumph of **Joshua 1:7-8**:

> "Only be strong and very *courageous*; be careful to do [everything] in accordance with the entire law (in our Bible) which Moses My servant commanded you; *do not* turn from it to the right or to the left, so that you may prosper *and* be successful wherever you go. This Book of the Law shall *not depart* from your mouth, but you shall read [and meditate on] it, *day, and night*, so that you may be careful to do [everything] in accordance with all that is written in it; for then you will make your way *prosperous*, and then you **will** be successful."

A Slow Awakening

With these truths now biblically affirmed, I aim to aid others by sharing my post-salvation journey—should anyone like to find the purpose and application of His Word in our daily life. For decades, casual reading yielded no such shift. Back then, I believed that Joshua's charge was exclusive to him, not me, or any other Christian—an impossible feat for mere mortals, unlike epic figures like Joshua. "Meditating day and night" seemed like rocket science to me. Yet, consistently reading His Book cover-to-cover for years *transformed* that view and my own spiritual domain, unveiling "impossibilities" as totally possible in Him (**Matthew 19:26; Mark 10:27; Luke 1:37**).

Believe What You Read, Not Read What You Believe

Resolving to revamp my study habits, I began reading the Bible annually, then—mind blown after a couple years—every six months for the past decade. Astonishingly, meditating on His Word day and night became instinctive, effortless—like breathing—without any deliberate intent. Outlandish? Not at all, but it's now second nature to me. How? Not by my will—it's a miracle, His Spirit weaving the Word stored in my mind over years, reshaping me from *within*. Think of it as in "garbage in, garbage out," or "we are what we eat" or for that matter, what we *think* (**Proverbs 23:7**). **Romans 12:2** nails it:

> "**Do not** be *conformed* to this world [any longer with its super-ficial values and customs] but **be transformed** and *progres-sively* changed [as you mature spiritually] by the **renewing** of *your mind* [focusing on godly values and ethical attitudes], so that you may *prove* [*for yourselves*] what the *will of God is*, that which is good and acceptable and perfect [in His *plan and purpose* for you]."

Early Emptiness

Initially, after salvation, nothing clicked because I lacked His Word being planted and rooted **within** me. Sporadic reading—passages here and there over decades—bore no depth or intimacy, all because I deemed spending time in His Word as unimportant. Like King Saul, I didn't value **Joshua 1:8-9** command, or **Isaiah 28:23; 55:10-11**—just a "reading" as recommended by church leaders. Good intent, flawed execution—lacking the Spirit's tools.

A Map of A Perfect Plan

Have you noticed how all these Scriptures quoted so far, when knitted together, paints a picture on the canvas of God's salvation plan? If so, bravo—I didn't either, until now.

From Casual to Convinced

Early on, my scant Word knowledge in me, yielded nothing. Casual glances over the Word—for decades—bred no knowledge or bond with Him. I dismissed all of those gains promised in the **Joshua 1:8-9**, and those of Isaiah's, *assuming their impossibility*—until **Matthew 19:26** corrected me:

> "With people [as far as it **depends** on them] it is **impossible,** but **with God all things are possible.**"

Religion demands your effort for what only God can do. **2 Timothy 4:3** alerts us why we are looking for "easy fixes":

> "The time will come when people ***will not*** tolerate **sound doctrine and accurate instruction** [that challenges them with God's **truth**]; but wanting to have their ears tickled [with something pleasing], they will *accumulate* for themselves [**many**] **teachers** [one after another, chosen] to satisfy their own desires and to ***support the errors*** they hold."

The Goldilocks Faith

Let's consider the last 1,800 years—with the sheep skipping from sect to sect, and like Goldilocks, in search of for "just the right church"? Early on, I saw that my brethren's prayer requests and chats mirrored my own lack of experiencing His promises and blessings. It dawned slowly—where most if not all of our woes stemmed **from us**, not from bogus "trials" sent from Him to the faithful, according to the hierarchy—a warped notion from the religious minds where, a Loving Father would send a vicious spiritual thug to *assess* "our loyalty" to Him, engendered by a ***misinterpretation*** and ***misrepresentation*** of the Book of Job.

Why do we bring our own "trials"? Would it surprise you to discover that it's because in our daily conduct, we **insist on doing** our *own* **will** over His own, ignoring the commands in His Word? The distorted story of Job fueled this myth of God "sending" a defeated life as either a "trial," or punishment to the faithful, forgetting that God, in His infinite Wisdom has engendered a ***consequence***, ***every time*** we violate His Laws.

John 16:32-33 refutes:

> "I have told you these things, so that **in Me** you **may have** [***perfect***] **peace**. In the world you have tribulation, distress, *and* suffering, but **be courageous** [be confident, be undaunted, be filled with joy]; ***I have overcome the world***" [My conquest is ***accomplished***, My **victory** abiding.]"

Isn't it strange how easily we miss little phrases when we read His Word like in here, "***may have***"? He gave us His Peace (**John 14:27; 16:33; 20:21**), just the same as the faith we already have, but it's up to us to seize it by our ***obedience***, not by wishful thinking. That's why He doesn't say "you have peace," but that **you may** have it. He is placing that responsibility of acquiring it, squarely on our shoulders.

Victory Assured

Please, consider what more can He do, short of force-feeding us with His sure promises? Our Victory's is **already won**—no sermon checklist adds to it. We just have to obey, just as in the Sinai wilderness, and choosing to join Johsua and Caleb and be the **exception**, rather than the rule.

A Fresh Lens

Now, this may have happened by mere chance, but one day, meditating on this **Joshua 1:8** passage, I slowed down my reading and caught eye on what He, **firsthand** said, not what I "though" He said, and discovered what He is really saying to Joshua and to us today, and it's right there, in the verse itself, in plain view, which is:

> "But you ***shall read*** (His Word), [and **meditate** on] it, ***day and night***."

He's not asking us to memorize it at all—just to **read it**. Meditation follows naturally. I had missed this, in reading my Bible randomly like a novel without order, a common religious habit.

No Excuses Today

Abundant Resources

Unlike Old Testament times—lacking Bibles, public media, and the Spirit's indwelling—***we stand without excuse***. They had fewer tools, yet from Genesis to Malachi, many were amazingly victorious by obeying His Word—others, faltered by doing the opposite with grave consequences. We must heed His instructions ***meticulously*** to reap the blessing. Next time you build a multipart toy, skim the assembly manual haphazardly—see how much you enjoy your trinket then.

Chronological Insight

When reading a book, we all follow a universal sequence, not cherry-picking here and there, and ***not*** grasping the story told, and its ***narrative thread***. Yet I—and millions—do exactly that with our Bible reading. Doubt me? Ask ten churchgoing Christians how often they've read His Book cover-to-cover. Finding one or even two would stun me.

No one reads novels randomly, yet this is the norm for church going folks, not the exception, when reading Scripture. It's easier now than ever—unlike Old Testament saints, unlettered, without printed Bibles, internet, or inspirational books, or with an indwelling Spirit. Nothing has changed since ancient times, one **must adhere**

strictly to His directives and Word to obtain His intended outcome and reward.

Lessons from Failures

This personal deduction shouldn't shock us at all—Old Testament figures, with fewer resources than us, stumbled plenty but later overcame by simple repentance and obedience. The worst king ever, Manasseh, the son of Zedekiah being a prime example. Take King Saul, who typify today's Christians whereby, every Jewish king received a copy of the Law Book to be **read** by him, **everyday** (**2 Kings 11:12**) in order to govern. And what is our governance today? Our *own daily personal lives* before Him.

But there is more, read Saul's rise to kingship and tally the years before he, and only because he was cornered, built an altar to God out of desperation—not devotion. Contrast this with Abraham, Isaac, Jacob, and David. Saul's self-absorption, like many believers today, spared no time or cared for God's Word. Plain and simple.

Living Joshua's Way

What rules lead us to fulfill **Joshua 1:7-8** today? Start with any Scripture that interest you, pray for affirmation, and assess *your* obedience to **John 14:26, 15:26,** and **16:13** and then just allow Him to take you to the next step. This process is unique to each one of us and therefore, no two would be alike or the same. In my walk, compliance yields Joshua's thriving life—meditating on His Word day and night, effortlessly. I've lived it. Note His earnest promise in **Isaiah 54:13**, defining us as **disciples**, not mere "**believers**," backed by the witness verses that follows.

In fifty years living as a Christian, no preacher, pastor, or teacher—across books, churches, TV, internet, or radio—has anyone hinted at how to experience meditating on God's Word day and night—**not one**—in your own personal life. Just how valuable do you think it is, being able to meditate on His Word perpetually? Yet, per His promise in **Psalm 127:1-2**, He **will fulfill** this feat in *your* *own life* that crafts **disciples** as pledged in **Matt. 10:24-25, John 14:26** and in **16:13**.

The Spirit's Sole Role

God has ordained His Spirit—*and He alone*—as the sheep's **sole** Teacher and Discipler, declaring this unequivocally in **Isaiah 54:13**:

> "And **ALL** (not some, or many, but **all**) your [**spiritual** (excludes our flesh)] sons (being born again by Messiah) **WILL** be *disciples* [of the Lord], and great will be the well-being of your sons."

Note His vow is that: "**all** *will be disciples*," **not** "*believers*." Why? Old Testament folk weren't individually Spirit-indwelt or deemed to be God's children, as in son or daughter, merely His people:

> "Then I will take you as *my people* (not as His children), and I will be your God (not your Father); and you will know that I am the Lord your God, who redeemed you and brought you out from under the burdens of Egypt." (**Exodus 6:7**).

Isaiah 54:13 envisions us—as future born-again **disciples**— not casual enthusiasts or church-defined "believers." This New Testament status stands firm today as on Pentecost Day.

Confirmed by Prophecy

He reaffirms this entirely and absolutely in **Ezekiel 34:20-23**:

> "Therefore, thus says the Lord God to them, 'Behold, I **Myself** (not a pastor, church, or religion) **will** judge between the [well-fed] fat sheep and the lean sheep. Because you push with side and shoulder, and gore with your horns all those that have become weak *and* sick until you have scattered them away, therefore, **I will** rescue My flock, and they shall no longer be prey; and I will judge between one sheep [ungodly] and another [godly]. Then I will appoint over them **ONE** *shepherd* and **He**

(again, not a pastor, teacher, or preacher) **will feed** *them*, [by a ruler like] My servant David (our Lord Jesus, the promised descendant through His Holy Spirit in **John 14:18**); *He will feed them and be their shepherd.*"

If this One Shepherd system is grasped and **lived** by every New Testament child of God, what's the outcome? **Jeremiah 31:33-35** answers that:

"But **this is the covenant** (our New Covenant today) which I will make with the house of Israel after **those days**, says the Lord, I will *put My law* **within** *them*, (through the Holy Spirit per the John scriptures cited above), and **I** *will* **write it** (not your pastor or religion) on **their hearts**;(**no** pastor or religion **will**, or **can EVER** do this); and **I will be** their God, and *they will be My people*. And **each man** will no longer teach his neighbor and his brother, saying, 'Know the Lord,' for they will **ALL know ME** [through **personal** experience], from the least of them to the greatest, says the Lord. For I will forgive their wickedness, and I will no longer remember their sin."

Lost Practice

Our Lord verifies this truth in **Matthew 23:8**, **John 6:45**, and **Hebrews 1:2**, about this God-sourced system—that **excludes** human institutions—but it **is not being taught** to new converts. Why? My only guess is that it might threaten the clergy's self-perceived roles, influence, or control over the sheep. Harsh? **Matthew 7:16** guides us to make this determination:

"By their **fruit** you will recognize them [that is, by their contrived doctrine and self-focus]."

Verse **20** seals it:

"Therefore, by their fruit you will *recognize* them [for *who* they are]."

Spiritual Famine

My spiritual barrenness revealed my teaching's inadequacy and scarceness. That's when I decided to cutoff the religious middleman, and submitting back to the Scripture's basics—to be guided by His Spirit, not men.

I tried sharing these truths with others, but one tends to become either an annoyance, or a perceived "threat" to those in charge (**Acts 4:19**). Tolerated or ignored? Didn't matter to me, I just couldn't ignore and abide with error, being disguised as "God's Word." I've since stepped out of that scene for Him to fulfill His **personalized** plan for me.

Spirit's Direct Line

John 14:26 and **16:1**, may sound like a broken record, but it details His approach and process for *implementing* His **Isaiah 54:13**'s promise into our lives:

> "But when He, the Spirit of Truth, comes, *He will **guide** you* into **ALL** the truth [the full and ***complete*** truth] (***not*** a part of it, but **all** of it, leaving **nothing** in between for **any** religious claim of having their *own truth*). For He will not speak on His own initiative (as in our churches), but He will speak whatever He hears [**from** the Father—the message regarding the Son], and He will disclose to you what is to come [in the future]."
>
> (The kind of **truth** that is **not** just a **part**, of it, but the **whole** of it, leaving **no room** for *any* religious pretensions that each one of them has **their own** "truth").

Now the question is, do you want God's Truth, or that from man? With this Spirit-to-spirit channel—not through men's filter—which will I choose? Knowing which one is **His** will, doesn't take much to figure this out, does it not? —His, not one from a denomination, cult, or sect—that alone *settles* it.

My Personal Change

For me, it was easy to see my spiritual poverty as a result of faulty teaching. I just had to take the necessary steps to pursue His plans for me. In **John chapters 14, 15,** and **16,** He explains how the promise of **Isaiah 54:13** was going to be implemented to fulfill in us, His promise to making us disciples, with a system where the change ***bubbles up from within***, not from without like in the case of the priests of Israel, whose system have been copied by all religions today.

He has Done It ALL Already

God has completed **everything** for us, as **Hebrews 4:3** declares:

> "His **works** were **completed** from the **foundation** of the world [**waiting** for **all** (those) who would **believe**]."

Countless times, I've heard public prayers—including my own in early years—pleading, "God, please help me change my life." It's as absurd as begging someone who hands you a cup of water and then begging for their help to swallow it. Ludicrous, yet that was me, ignorant of His Word and will.

It's a Personal Choice

The solution to this quandary lies within our reach—it's intimate, discretionary, and it's a matter between God and the new convert. I can assure anyone—**obeying** Him to the best of my ability, revolutionized my Christian walk and daily existence, irrevocably. This shift ignited after years of drifting, wrestling with insecurity, discontent, and even doubting about my own salvation's reality—especially against **John 10:10**'s promise that my life was to be **different** than that of the rest of the world. Today, He is my witness that my life is not only different, but revolutionary!

My revolution began in the early 2010's when one day, abruptly, while pondering about my forty years of fruitless Bible reading, a question surfaced—"As a young lad, how did you read ***Paradise***

Lost?" It wasn't mocking—just a curious inquiry. The answer dawned instantly—from start to finish, as any book demands.

From Chaos to Clarity

That revelation exposed my folly—forty years of dart-throwing Scripture reading, missing the mark, or more like flinging scriptural spaghetti at a wall to see what stuck. Grasping this madness, I sensed the question's divine origin—though I can't swear to it.

Since then, I've read His Word daily, sequentially, from **Genesis 1:1** to the very last word in **Revelation 22**'s closing chapter. I crafted a system that fit me. Should you choose this path, I'll share mine—not as if this is the only way, but a to spark one of your own—to align with **Joshua 1:7-8**, and every other treasure in His Book.

My Method Unveiled

Here's how I began, not insisting that you mimic—I tallied the Bible's 1,189 chapters, divided by 365 days (3.25 daily), rounded to 4—two chapters from each Testament:

Day one: Genesis 1-2, Matthew 1-2.
Day two: Genesis 3-4, Matthew 3-4.
Day three: Genesis 5-6, Matthew 5-6.
And so on.

In eleven months, I finished the whole Bible and restarted the same process the next day. Thereabouts by year three or four, I upped it to four Old Testament and three New Testament chapters, reading His Manual twice yearly ever since. My life's **never been the same**, I solemnly promise yours won't be either.

What Salvation is vs. The Kingdom's

I had my first epiphany around 2013, and it was that salvation **does not grant** a believer automatically, our entry into His Kingdom. If one is unaware about this truth, how could then anyone seek it (**Matthew 6:33**)? This spurred a quest (**Proverbs 25:2**), which was clarified in **John 9:39**'s Greek nuance:

"Then Jesus said, 'I came into this world (not just for *universal salvation*, but also) for **judgment** [to **separate** **those** (today's church going people) who **believe in Me** (talking to **Christians**, *not the lost*) from those who **reject** Me (**Hosea 4:6**: being a **priest** to Him)—to **declare** (the **Hosea 4:6**) judgment on those who **choose** to be **separated** from God (to be His priest)], so that the sightless would see, and those who see would become *blind* .'"

There is a veiled message (**Prov. 25:2**) in this passage, besides the obvious outer meaning to the Pharisees and Sadducees which is manyfold. Our perceived idea that He came to die on a cross **only** to save humanity, is shattered by His clear message that He is talking to **only to those who believe in Him**, not to the children of Satan who will *always* persecute the godly (do read **Ezek. 24:38**; **1 John:3:12**; **Jude 1:11**). I know, this was still also hard for me to absorb this truth bomb myself, and needed more confirmation, and I got it, when I looked up the Greek word translated as "**judgment**," which actually means:

a). Condemnation of a *wrong*, a *decision* [whether severe or mild].

b). A matter to be *judicially decided*.

c). The *sentence* of a judge

As we can readily see, this has **nothing to do** with the Final Judgement, but about something that Peter refers to in **1 Peter 4:17** where:

"For it is the time [destined] for **judgment** to *begin* with the *household* of God (the Judgement Seat of Christ in **2 Corinthians 5:10**) and if *it* begins with us, what will the outcome be for those who do not respect *or* believe *or* obey the gospel of God?

Division Among Kin

In **Matthew 13:55** He shows us His own family's split—only James and Jude followed, not Joseph, Simon, or at least two sisters we know of. But what about being blind? Oh yes, He pointed out that this is going on today, right inside our churches where the sheep *is not* aware about the *difference* between being *just saved* from His *Wrath*, and that of *being saved from His Wrath* and **entering** the kingdom. This blindness still persists in churches today; the sheep is totally unaware about what salvation actually is, and what the Kingdom stands for.

And still, He wasn't done yet, He pointed out what the nature of the Division is—**Matthew 10:34-37** elaborates:

> "Do not think that I have come to bring peace on the earth; I have not come to bring peace, but a sword [of **division** between **belief** and **unbelief** of His Word]. For I have come to set a man **against** his father, and a daughter against her mother, and a daughter-in-law against her mother-in-law; and a man's ene-mies will be the *members of his* [**own**] *household* [when one believes (His Word by **their actions**) and another does not]. He who loves father or mother more than Me is not worthy of Me (being in His Presence); and he who loves son or daughter more than Me is not worthy of Me (anything that **overrides** our obedience)."

This brings an interesting question, if only "*believing*" does the salvation thing, why would that divide a Chrisitan family? Let that sink in—why would He tells us that a there would be two kinds of followers within the Body of Christ? Well, weren't there also **two groups** in the saved multitude out of Egypt, who believed the Gospel of Moses? One group (Joshua and Caleb) believed what God said *through* Moses (our Spirit now in us), and the other group rejected it. One is free to believe that this is simply, just another "coincidence" or, given all the evidence presented so far, can one begin to connect the dots?

Like in Exodus, our Bible mirrors the written Ten Commandments, Moses symbolizing the Spirit teaching His Word and the saved slaves—like today's church—were **divided**—only Joshua and Caleb trusted God's Word; the others didn't.

God's Teaching Way, or Man's?

Can we now detect the glaring contradiction between God's way of teaching the *meaning* of His Word (see **Psalm 91:16**), and that of men's methods through the religious establishment with their church complex?

Of course, these disclosures hit me right between the eyes of my *old understanding* and stunned me. I immediately asked for even more confirmation, clarification, and understanding, and it came. This division is specific to the **family**, *not* about the saved and unsaved since the world is **already divided between** the seeds of Cain vs Seth.

In another words, if we don't know His Word *through* His Spirit, *we won't understand it clearly*, nor will we comprehend or appreciate His plan for each one of us. So, even though we are saved, we potentially are *still blind* to His Word as He warned the Jews in **Isaiah 6:10**; **29:9-10** and other scriptures.

Spirit-Led Reading

This spiritual blindness is the result of being without the tutoring of His Spirit (**Isaiah 6:8-10**; **29:9-10**), I shifted—reading as it is written, unfiltered, and bypassing my intellect, letting it sink in a distraction-free mental state. Reflecting on what's been read later, with insights emerging on their own—not mine, but His Spirit's work. It's unique to each one of us—you can draw your own conclusions here, because I deem this phase to be highly personal.

A Mind Transformed

God tailors His system of instruction and dove tails it to our level of comprehension and spiritual experience—unlike we do with other people by nature. This routine of consistently reading His Word and allowing His Spirit to do His work, mimics the programming of a computer—reading the inputted data, (the eyes as keyboard), then store them (our memory as RAM) into our spirit conscience/mind (our operating system), to decode them either without the help from anyone else or, with that of a pastor, or some general spiritual guru—before Jesus Christ, these were the *only options* for humans—but after the cross, we have the Comforter sent by our Father who over time, will translate, interpret, and reveal the lessons that He *wrote* Himself, into **your own** spirit without any effort.

This is what **Romans 12:2** is all about:

> "And *do not* be **conformed** to this world [any longer with its superficial values and customs] but **be transformed** and progressively **changed** [as you mature spiritually] by the **renewing** of **your** *mind* [focusing on godly values and ethical attitudes], so that you may prove [for yourselves] what the will of God is, that which is good and acceptable and perfect [*in His plan and purpose for you*]."

Then, another interesting question arises, what are **you** going *to program* **into** that O/S **inside your spirit**? Is it going to be God's Truth that we can use for our benefit, or the live streaming World's Entertainment Wheel of Fortune from the world, so that they can *use against us*? Our choice, no one else's. It's curious how a tapestry of verses woven together paints a living river flowing within, per **John 7:38**:

> "He, who believes in Me [who **adheres** to, **trusts** in, and **relies** on Me], as the Scripture has said, 'From his **innermost** being will flow **continually** (as in meditating day and night), rivers of living water' " (see **John 6:63**).

The Gospels echo this sentiment—water associated to His Word (in **John 4**, and in **chapter 15**).

A Renewed Bond

Now, once I started building on this foundation (**Matthew 7:24; 1 Corinthians 3:11; Ephesians 2:20**), all the knowledge gaps that existed in my understanding between the correlation of our mind, spirit, His Word, and His Spirit, have been filled—my closeness with Him **became real**, surpassing 1975's first spark that ignited it. Unthinkable back then, but now, a reality. It's like travel—you don't grasp a place's beauty in other countries, until you go there. Thus, I reaped, one of many being the life of **John 10:10**'s benefits, and stunningly, received **Psalm 91**'s treasures as well, especially that final promise in **Psalm 91:16** as quoted below.

Life Overflowing

My heart brims with joy and thanksgiving ever since I saw and started to experience the width and length and **height** and depth of His love (**Eph. 3:18**) verbalized in all its glory in **Psalm 91** that ends with:

> "With a long life I will satisfy him, and I *will let him* **SEE** My salvation" (**Psalm 91:16**).

And another one in **Isaiah 58:8**:

> "Then *your light* will break out like the dawn, and your healing (restoration, new life) will quickly spring forth; your righteousness will go before you [leading you to peace and prosperity], and the glory of the Lord *will be* your *rear guard*."

And it doesn't end there because God has already **secured it all**, as **Psalm 91:16** above promises. But the cherry on top is in **Isaiah 65:24** which seals it:

> "It shall also come to pass that *before* they call, I **will** answer; and while they are still speaking, I **will** hear."

An Unseen Shift

Reflect on this: this inner transformation defies explanation—no fanfare, no markers, it simply unfolds all on its own. **Luke 17:20-21** explains, and validates it:

> "Now having been asked by the Pharisees when the **kingdom of God** would come, He replied, 'The kingdom of God is not coming with signs to be observed *or* with a visible display; nor will people say', 'Look! Here it is!' or 'There it is!' For **the king-**

dom of God is <u>inside</u> YOU [because of **<u>My presence</u>** (in the form of the Holy Spirit)].”

Jesus echoes this to Nicodemus in **John 3:8**:

“The wind blows where it wishes and you hear its sound, but you **do not know** where it is coming from, and where it is going; so, it is with **<u>everyone</u>** who is **<u>born of the Spirit</u>**.”

His Strength, Our Trust

God will **<u>never demand</u>** from us something that *we can't do*—He alone can, *when and if*, we “*adhere to*, *trust in*, and *rely*” on Him. Nevertheless, it's crucial to accept and understand that **<u>nothing happens</u>** *without our active partnership* with His Spirit. . This renewal (**Romans 12:2**) thrives only through Him, as **Psalm 127:1** warns:

“*<u>Unless</u>* the Lord *<u>builds</u>* the house, they *<u>labor in vain</u>* who build it; unless the Lord guards the city, the watchman keeps awake *<u>in vain</u>*”

Zechariah 4:6 doubles down:

“*<u>Not</u>* by might, nor by power, but *<u>by My Spirit</u>* says the Lord of hosts” (**Zech. 4:6**).

No Shortcuts Allowed

Framing this in human terms, yet seeing it through His lens, demands rigor—His Word brooks no disobedience or bypasses. It's *His way or nothing*, **<u>not</u>** from unwillingness, but because of spiritual laws—Adam **<u>ceded all of his authority</u>** bestowed to him **<u>by God</u>** to Satan (**Genesis 1:28; Psalm 138:2; Mark 13:31; Luke 16:17**, and in **21:33**; and **John 10:35**).

God won't **breach** His Word that **<u>He gave to Adam</u>**, not even for the love of His children living in his world. Why, is God powerless? Not at all! He gave **<u>YOU</u>** **<u>every tool</u>** you will need to **<u>overcome</u>**

every obstacle that the devil will put in front of you—the only problem is, like in the Sinai Desert, you **MUST** obey *His commands*!

This alone <u>settles</u> that silly and age-old ludicrous and laughable question: "Why does God allows evil in this world." Some may see me as harsh, but I align it with **John 10:34**:

"If He called them gods, men to whom the Word of God came [and the Scripture (God's Word) cannot be <u>undone</u>, <u>annulled</u>, or <u>broken</u>."

If that rule applies to the Word given to Adam, it applies to us today, as well. And equally important in **Deuteronomy 8:3**, and echoed in **Matthew 4:4**:

> "But He answered and said, 'It is written, Man shall *not live* by bread alone, but by <u>**every Word**</u> (not man's religion) that *proceeds* <u>*from*</u> the Mouth of God' (our Bible)."

Chapter Four

Only One Spokesman

Mimicking the Real

It would not be outlandish to state that in today's Christianity—denominations, sects, cults—that they are just merely duplicating a form of the Old Testament idol worship that the Jews found themselves doing, when they introduced the worship of the Canaanite's gods in their religious culture, as seen in the Book of Judges, after Jushua's generation passed on—except that today, instead of a High Priest, we find a pope, a president, archbishops, Imam's, etc., and instead of Levites, priests, pastors, preachers, clerics—and just like them, have *diverged from the truth of His Word*, *the first-century church worship order*, and *Jesus' way of life teachings*, into a mix of a religious Tower of Babel.

This new religious system was born in the third century as the Catholic church which shifted, under pagan Caesar's control and influence, the Christian faith, and reshaped the Way of Life that He left us, into a Babylonian style corner edifice we have come to know as "churches." It is now just an imitation of the Jewish model, and system of worship that Jesus condemned (**Matthew 23**; **Luke chapters 6**, **10**, and **11**). Yet, it was *Christ's model that Christianity defeated Rome*, not Israel with its religion—and Satan, failing to crush it (**Matthew 16:18**) with persecution, infiltrated and subverted it, trading <u>discipleship</u> for "**believer-ship**," and the Chirstian Way of Life, for a pagan look alike religion. However, we must always remember that there will *always be* a remnant faithful to His Word, and His ways.

A Historical Parallel

I sought a biblical allegory for this change in the apostolic model, to the modern era church system, which erased Jesus' Legacy—a facsimile of the Christian way of life and His Word principles, attractively packaged in religion—run by a religious machine, akin to the worldly pagan systems of old—only that this one has a veneer of a Christian façade.

Israel's post-Moses apostasy mirrors it—God's will, swapped for tradition.

Judaism also began as a **way of life** under Moses, based on the Word of God, and was corrupted when Israel rejected His Covenant and rule while Joshua was still in charge, and who was later **replaced** by judges, prophets, and ultimately, by kings (**1 Samuel 8:4-7**), yearning to integrate, resemble, and live like the pagans. And sure enough, this same change took place in Christianity as well, and by the third century, as if prophesied by Him in the story **1 Samuel 8:4-7**.

Protestantism birthed a new era of multiple "kings" with numerous new kinds of "pope" types, save the title—Quakers, Baptists, Mormons, Presbyterians—tweaked echoes of the Catholic mold, now gone universal.

Gospels' Warning

The Gospels and New Testament writings prophesied this distortion—like in the Old Testament, it bred a religion that ultimately, razed to the ground the nation of Israel in 70 A.D.—personally ruinous for them then, and for us today. This development was written solely to reveal to the N.T. Church saints, about men's religious failure in the **absence of His presence and Truth (Romans 15:4; 1 Corinthians 10:11**), they underscore the **necessity** and the **purpose** for His Spirit's **indwelling** in us.

The ignorance of the sheep allowed men to **exchange** a divine teaching model *superior to that of the Apostles* where, they had Him to themselves only on waking hours—we have Him **24/7**—without the *spiritual* unawareness, any mediation, and interference of religious men.

Just as a reminder, let's contrast the choice of the Apostle Matthias (*man-chosen*) with that of Paul (*God-chosen, Spirit-filled*)—this is the gap and divergence between man's religion and their churches, and a **Spirit-led life**. Man's stubbornness races and takes you *nowhere*—Jesus left a **way of life**, not a corner building, nor needs the *teaching services* of a religious middleman (see **Matt. 23:8-10; John 3-2**, and in **13:14**).

Israel's Echo

Israel proved beyond any reasonable doubt that religion **doesn't work**—nor do today's thousands of its variants. Why else send His Spirit to reside in each one of us? Common sense, lost since the third century, should scream this truth to us. My issue after my conversion wasn't about the Christian faith, but the thickness of the religion's veil that distorts its truth.

I am not portraying nor defining here, a "new" Christianity—just the **biblical alignment** for those who are open to shed their religious establishment baggage, *transform* their mind, and start truly *walking with Him* by seeking the kingdom first, per **Matthew 6:33** and how it develops in chapter **19:26**:

> "But Jesus looked at them and said to them, 'With men this is *impossible*, but with God **all** things are *possible*'."

And **Mark 9:23** adds:

> "Jesus said to him, 'If **you** can **believe**, **all** things are **possible** to him *who* **believes**'." (See also **10:27**).

Living Stones, Not Bricks

Deeper Word knowledge bears fruit—which is <u>**stifled**</u> by congregational molds. Churches craft uniform bricks (**Isaiah 65:3**; **Exodus 20:25**), not the <u>**unique**</u> living stones that we are *meant* to be:

> "You [believers], like ***living stones***, are being built up into a <u>**spiritual house**</u> for a holy and dedicated **PRIESTHOOD**, to offer spiritual sacrifices [that are] acceptable and pleasing to God through Jesus Christ" (**1 Peter 2:4-5**).

God seeks individuals, not clones. Post-Moses and Joshua, Israel's way became religious—so too, has Christ's Church become post-apostles.

Samuel's Lesson

The **1 Samuel 8:4-7** episode illustrates this parallel template:

> "Then all the elders of Israel gathered together and came to Samuel at Ramah and said to him, 'Look, you have grown old, and your sons do not walk in your ways. Now appoint us a king to judge us [and ***rule*** over us] like all the ***other nations***.' But their demand displeased Samuel when they said, 'Give us a king to ***judge and rule*** over us.' So, Samuel prayed to the Lord. The Lord said to Samuel, 'Listen to the voice of the people in regard to all that they say to you, for they have ***not <u>rejected</u> you***, but they **have <u>rejected</u>** Me from being King over them."

God equaled Samuel's presence as His own manifestation in the midst of Israel—prophets prefiguring the ***Spirit's role in His New Testament Church*** (**<u>people</u>, not <u>buildings</u>**). This interpretation was behind the ruling class idea, that kings could play the role of "gods" under Rome's papacy, who had <u>**usurped**</u>, not only the Father's Throne, but ***Christ position itself***, until Napoleon's 1800s reckoning.

The Final Prophet

Why document all of this? Well, if the O.T. was written for "*our instruction*," then *all of these passages* are relevant, and it should reveal to us today, how to **identify** Who is **the only designated Spokesman and Prophet** by God Himself—**Jesus**—for these last days, per **Hebrews 1:1-2**:

> "God, having **_spoken_** to the fathers long ago in [the **_voices and writings_** of] the **_prophets_** in many separate revelations [each of which set forth a portion of the truth], and in many ways, **_has in these last days SPOKEN_** [**_with finality_**] **to US** in [the person of **_ONE_** who is, by His character and nature] **His Son** [namely Jesus], whom He **appointed** heir and **lawful** owner of **all things**, **_through_** whom also He created the universe [that is, the universe as a space-time-matter continuum]."

Unless we listen to His Word *through* His Spirit, with *seriousness and obedience*, God's decree leaves *no room for doubt*— His Son, Jesus Christ, is His **only spokesman** in this universe, not denominational voices, sects, churches, or religious groups.

The Sole Spokesman

Christ's Authority

Unless we are *willing to listen and obey His Word* with all seriousness, God's track record of *executing* His judgments, dependability, and dealings with mankind, leaves no doubt—His Son, Christ Jesus has been named to be **His sole personal Representative** to all humanity living in this **entire universe**—**NOT** to **any** other voices from denominational sects, churches, or religious groups.

This being a fact, **Hebrews 1:1-2** poses a pivotal question: Just whom, did the Son **appoint** to be **His SOLE earthly voice and Representative** to man, after returning to the Father?

John 14:26 answers this as **clear** as a crystal:

"But the Helper (Comforter, Advocate, Intercessor—Counselor, Strengthener, Standby), *__the Holy Spirit__*, whom the Father will send in My name [in *__My place__*, to *__represent Me__* and __ACT__ on My behalf], __He__ (__not__ your denomination, religion, or pastors) will teach __you__ __ALL__ things (this excludes, again, *__all and any__* religious group, sect, or denomination). And He will help you *__remember everything__* that I have told you."

(Of course, this is __limited only__ to *those* of us who are willing to *listen* and *obey*)."

Spirit Over Religion

What should leap out to any believer, who is sadly Word illiterate, and has chosen religion over His Spirit? Yes, just how can His Spirit "help you to remember" His Word (read **Rev. 19:13**), if it's __not__ known, or inside you? The clarity of **Hebrews 1:1-2**, and John **14:26** is not veiled, nor unclouded—is aligned with the Scriptures that paints an unmistakable portrait of the One whom *we* __must listen__ to and __obey__ every Word that comes out of His mouth. No room exists to dodge or evade this truth.

Now, contextualize this with **1 Samuel 8:4-7**, we look at the perfect example of what happened to the Christian faith after the apostles—in the third century, Christians accepted a king in the form of a pope, whom they could see with their eyes and hear with their ears—a human idol together with a man-made religion—now they could be equal with the rest of the pagans in the Roman world, who worshipped in temples and on mountains—the same thing Jesus rejected when He spoke to the Samaritan woman (**John 4**)—Pagan echoes in Catholicism? Yes, it's undeniable—I saw it and experienced myself, as a child.

Rejecting His Order

Our changeless God views this third century shift just as He did Israel's king-demand in Samuel's days—a **rejection** of His Spirit's primacy (**John 14:26**; and in **16:13**). Substituting a religious proxy for His appointed Teacher, mimics the Jews' choice against Samuel.

Excuses won't sway Him—consequences loom—lost inheritance and rewards (**1 Corinthians 3:15**; **Galatians 3:18**, and in **4:30**; **Ephesians 1:14**; **Revelation 22:12-15**). Opting for a denominational voice over His Spirit—*intentional or not*—echoes Samuel's yardstick—a **rejection** of God's plan and purpose. No doubt, in the desert, the Jews didn't see it that way either, but there they still are, their bones buried in the wilderness.

His Unchanging Nature

This may jar some, but **Isaiah 55** declares that His thoughts and ways transcend ours. **1 Samuel 16:7** adds:

> "The Lord sees *not as man sees*; for man looks at the outward appearance, but the Lord *looks at the heart*."

And in **1 John 1:5**:

> "This is the message [of God's promised revelation] which we have heard **from** Him and now *announce* to **you**, that God is Light [He is holy, His message is truthful, He is perfect in righteousness], and in Him *there is* **no** darkness at all" (also **Job 34:21**).

For those who may not know, or are familiar with His Character, Nature, and Person, as revealed all over the Old, and New Testament, when it comes to Him there is, either a **yes**, or a **no**, it's **black** or **white**, **all in**, or **all out**; and there is *nothing else* in between.

His nature is absolute—per **Hebrews 13:8**:

> "Jesus Christ is **the same** yesterday, today, and **forever**."

Exodus as Our Mirror

Consider Exodus' Journey as the *physical representation* and parallel for the *spiritual journey* experienced by His Church in the New Testamen—saved from sin's slavery (*Satan as Pharaoh*), we trek the desert (***70-90 years in this world***, [**John 16:33**; **Acts 14:22**]) journeying toward the Promised Land (the life of **John 10:10** for us)—His Kingdom is ***spiritual for now*** (**Luke 17:20-21**)—Moses prefigures Jesus, Aaron his spokesman (**Exodus 4:14-16**) akin to the Spirit, leading us to conquer Canaan (***overcoming the world***, per **John 16:33**) in our quest for a **John 10:10**'s life.

Deuteronomy 6:10-11 reflects on the outcome for those who reach it:

> "Then it shall come about when the **Lord** your God (**not** you, your church, or your religion) **brings you** into the land which He swore (solemnly **promised**) to [give] your fathers—to Abraham (see **Galatians 3:29**), Isaac, and Jacob—to give you, [a land with] great and splendid cities which **you did not** build, and houses full of all good things which **you did not** fill, and hewn (excavated) cisterns (wells) which **you did not** dig out, and vineyards and olive trees which **you did not plant**".

1 Corinthians 15:57 echoes it:

> "Thanks be to God, who ***gives us*** the victory [as **conquerors**] **through** our Lord."

Everything is Done by Jesus, Nothing by Us

In Exodus, Moses symbolizes Jesus not only as a liberator, but also as someone who left Pharaoh's Palace to identify himself with the slaves, just as our Lord descended from His Father's Throne to identify Himself with the human race.

This parallel cannot be ignored. Aaron was then appointed as Moses' spokesman—another similarity to our Lord appointing the Holy Spirit as His Delegate. It is the same today, Jesus, leading the slaves of this world with the Spirit as His **only** Voice just as Aaron was (**Exodus 4:14-16**), as does the Spirit for us. They later conquered Canaan (we ***overcome*** the world to give us the life of **John 10:10**), the same goal as that of **Deuteronomy 6:10-11** mentioned above. He has **done it all**, not us, nor the religions.

The Kingdom is Not Hidden

Jesus, guiding us post-salvation, **knows** the Kingdom's locale. **Luke 17:20-21** reveals it:

> "Now having been asked by the Pharisees when the **kingdom of God** would come, He replied, 'The kingdom of God is **not** coming with signs to be observed *or* with a **visible** display; nor will people say, 'Look! Here it is!' or 'There it is!' For the kingdom of God is **within you** [**inside**]" (**Luke 17:20-21**).

Post-cross this with **John 14:26** and **16:13**—it's evident **Who's inside us**. And how do we reach the Promised Land, just like Joshua ad Caleb did? By our **Obedience**—practicing **Matthew 6:33**'s method, along with **John 14:6** and **16:13**'s as the path—lands us in the **John 10:10**'s life, our earthly and eternal goal until we die, or are taken up in the rapture.

Truth or Baiting?

Two conclusions emerge considering the combination of all these cited scriptures—He either spoke truth in all of these verses, or He tantalized us with unfulfilled promises. To doubt **any** of this, is to question **John 3:34**:

> "He, whom God has **sent speaks** the ***Words of God*** [proclaiming the Father's own ***message***]; for God ***gives*** the [***gift*** of the] ***Spirit*** without measure" (also, **Luke 4:18**).

You decide—ditch the religious middlemen as far as teaching God's Word, or grasp these Scriptures' scope, and like Joshua, we can challenge the nay sayers with **Joshua 24:15**:

> "If it is unacceptable in your sight to serve the Lord, choose for yourselves this day **whom** you will serve, whether the gods which your fathers served that were on the other side of the River, or the gods of the Amorites in whose land you live;

but *as for me* and my house, we *will serve* the Lord (**Joshua 24:14-15**).

Idols Unmasked

Before Joshua said this to his fellow Jews, he asked them to get rid of their idols. Back then, it wasn't easy to recognize *what my idols were* after being saved but I can recognize them today. They were my professional success, a fat bank account, spending 4 to 8 hours in front of the television, my sports hobbies, and other activities that *seemed harmless* to me because I didn't examined my motivations.

But, in fact, anything we are passionate about, and consider more important than **knowing Him** through His Word and His Spirit, and that comes before Him, or replaces Him, **is an idol**.

Story of Samuel Clarified

One needs to understand that the people's decision described in **1 Samuel 8:4-7**, **does not** mean that God **forsook**, **rejected**, or **abandoned** Israel—He noted their rejection of **His rule through Samuel**, and today for us. It's all about *rejecting His Spirit to guide us* as designed in favor for the **religious model**. Our salvation's secure (**Numbers 23:19**; **Romans 11:29**)—He won't return us to the world (**Deuteronomy 17:16**; **John 17:14-15**).

Therefore, everything we have covered so far in this discussion isn't about our salvation (**Joel 2:32**; **Acts 2:21**; **Romans 10:13**), but it's about the *fruit of our obedience*. Therefore, **ALL** of what we have been discussing here so far has **NOTHING** to do with how secure our salvation is. He clearly tells that **it is** assured, in **Joel 2:32**, **Acts 2:21** and in **Rom. 10:13**.

Furthermore, in **Numbers 23:19** He guarantees us that:

"God is **not** a man, that He should lie, Nor a son of man, that He should repent. Has He said, and will He not do it? Or has He spoken, and will He not *make it good* and **fulfill** it? (**Numb. 23:19**) also in **1 Samuel 15:28-30** and **Mal. 3:6**.

Wrath Averted

Also, as hashed out earlier, we *must clearly* understand *what* salvation *is*, and is *not*, but mainly that:

> "Therefore, since we have now been justified [declared **free** of the guilt of **sin**] by His blood, we will be **SAVED from the wrath of God** through Him" (also in **1 Thess. 1:10**, and **5:9**).

In the simplest terms, salvation *spares us the Final Judgment's wrath*—nothing more, nothing less. Pulpits often bundle salvation arbitrarily, with an automatic Kingdom entry, tied neatly with the bow of religious approval, not divine approbation.

Sorry, His Word disagrees about this and with **their assumption**—don't allow yourself to take you thirty years to find out and see this, as I did.

Exodus as Our Guide

Our call today *mirrors* that of the Exodus story—study **Numbers 2:1-29**'s encampment arrangement order. Which tribe dwelt **around** the tabernacle of His Presence? Yes, **only Levi's descendants**—none of the other eleven tribes were allowed to do this under the penalty of death. This array in the desert is a symbol of *who are the ones* **allowed** *to be dwelling* around the Tabernacle of the Heavenly Jerusalem (**Revelation 21:3**; and **22:12-15**), revealing **the dwelling** place for those **chosen from the many called**.

This is clearly referred to in **Hebrews 9:23-24**:

> "Therefore, it was necessary for the [earthly] **copies** of the *heavenly things* to be cleansed with these, but the heavenly things themselves required far better sacrifices than these. For Christ did not enter into a holy place made with hands, a **mere copy** of the true one [in heaven], but [He entered] into *heaven itself*, now to appear in the very presence of God on *our behalf*."

Only the obedient will camp there; others will face rejection (**Hosea 4:6; 2 Corinthians 13:5-6; Hebrews 12:17**). You can then see now that failing this test in **1 Corinthians 3:13-15** has <u>eternal consequences</u>.

It's One or the Other

His proposal then is (the reason why He wrote the Old Testament), is for us to reflect on that lesson from the Exodus story. Make no mistake—it will be the same around His Tabernacle in heaven (**Rev. 7:15; and 21:3**). It's an either/or situation—you will be there, or you will be ***rejected*** (**Hosea 4:6; 2 Corinthians 13:5-6; Hebrews 12:17**) and live <u>outside</u> the New Jerusalem (**Revelation 22:12-15**).

If anyone doubts this, just read the consequences in **1 Corinthians 3:13-15** and **2 Corinthians 13:5**—should you fail this test. Knowing now that living in His Presence in eternity is ***not part of our salvation***—which is free (**Romans 11:29** et al.)—then we must realize that we have to do something—**IF** we want to earn that inheritance as our reward for our faithful work (**Revelation 22:12-15; Psalm 19:11; Isaiah 40:10; 62:11; Jeremiah 31:16; 1 Corinthians 3:8; 3:14**).

Free Gift, Earned Reward

Undoubtedly, Salvation's free according to **Romans 11:29**:

> "For the ***favor*** [with which one receives without <u>any</u> merit of his own] and the ***calling*** of God (for salvation) ***are irrevocable***—[for He ***does not withdraw*** what He has **given**, ***nor*** does He change His mind about those to whom He gives His grace (for those who <u>respond</u> to the call), or to whom He sends <u>His call</u>."

Yet, Kingdom entry demands an <u>effort</u>—our faithful work that <u>qualifies</u> us to <u>receive</u> His reward (**Revelation 22:15; Psalm 19:11; Isaiah 40:10, and in 62:11; Jeremiah 31:16; 1 Corinthians 3:8, and in verse 14**).

Satan Tries to Steal This Reward

If something enters your mind that blocks these truths, just consider where it's coming from. Any attempt to *change our path to follow* God's plan **threatens** the enemy, who loves to rob us of the best eternal reward He has because of his hatred of God and His children.

However, entering the Kingdom **requires our effort**—for the reward of faithful work (**Revelation 22:12-15; Psalm 19:11; Isaiah 40:10 and 62:11; Jeremiah 31:16; 1 Corinthians 3:8 and verse 14**). Satan delights in blocking this amazing reward through **religious misdirection**, just as he did with Israel for fifteen centuries and with Christians for the past eighteen centuries, robbing God's children of the best He offers. This is his revenge against Him, for we matter nothing to him.

Disciples, Not Believers

The church's dilemma? Their teaching system *can only churn out* "**believers**," not proven **disciples** as Christ **commands** (**Matthew 28:19; John 8:31**, and in **15:8**). Disciples **overcome** the world **through** Him (**1 John 2:13**, and in **4:4**)—*not in our strength, but in His* (**John 16:33; Mark 9:24**). This demands **Word knowledge** that only He can provide (**John 13:10, 15:3**). Again, in **John 14:26** He reiterates to us:

> "But the Helper (***Comforter, Advocate, Intercessor— Counselor, Strengthener, Standby***), the Holy Spirit, whom the Father will send in My Name [***in My* PLACE**, to represent Me and **act** on My behalf], He will **teach** you **all** things (not some of them, as in your church, but **ALL**)."

Three Truths

a). The Spirit **mirrors** Jesus' *personal and physical presence*, teaching us today, just as He did with the Twelve (**Luke 10:1; John 6:66**).

b). **Without** God's Word **knowledge**, how can His Spirit remind you of His Words? Or the rules by which to **live our lives**.

c). **Choosing** men's teachings over His Spirit thwarts our experience of both—a and b.

Thus, being that all three are true, how can then, a churchgoer experience **Joshua 1:8-9**, **Psalm 91**, and even less, **John 10:10** in their *own lives*? It's pretty obvious, isn't it?

Living Under Grace is Not an Excuse

Living "under grace" isn't a free pass to ignore God's commands—Jesus **sees us** and *expects from us just the same* just as He did from Joshua, David, the twelve apostles, Paul, and a host of other Bible heroes. **John 17:6** proves this:

> "I have manifested Your Name [and ***revealed*** Your very self, Your **REAL SELF** (that is, through His *Word* while He was here)] to the people (the disciples, you, and I) whom You have ***given*** Me **out** of the world; they were Yours and You gave them to Me, and **they have kept** and **obeyed** Your **Word**."

No Exceptions

Missed the "kept and obeyed"? Once I did that myself, until I found His Spirit's illuminating His Word for me. I also once thought that "grace" excused this, imagining an Old Testament God *unlike* Jesus—until I came across **Exodus 23:20-22**:

> "Behold, I am going to **send** (like His Spirit today to us) an Angel (the **pre-incarnate Jesus**) before you to **keep and guard** you on the way and to **bring you** to the place I have prepared. Be on **your guard** before Him, **listen** to and **obey** His voice; **do NOT** be rebellious toward Him *or* provoke Him, for He **will not pardon** your transgression, since My Name (authority) is in Him. But if you will indeed **listen to and truly obey** His voice, and **do everything** that **I say**, then I will be an enemy to your enemies and an adversary to your adversaries."

Jesus Doesn't Change

If you think that Jesus is just benevolent, and that He will over-looks those failings **not washed** away by **1 John 1:9**, think again, for **Hebrews 13:8** assures us that:

"Jesus is **the same** yesterday, today, and forever."

And in **Exodus 23:20-21**, He doubles down about *how serious this is*:

> "Behold, I am going to send an Angel (pre-incarnate Jesus) before you to keep *and* guard you on the way and to bring you to the place I have prepared. *Be on your guard before Him*, **lis-ten** to *and* **obey** His voice; *do not* be rebellious toward Him *or* provoke Him, for **He will not pardon** your transgression, since My Name (authority) is in Him."

Yes, He will **never** leave us or forsake us, but He certainly expects you to do your part. If not, **Luke 9:23** and **John 15:2** are a joke, right? He certainly expects us to do **our part** (**Luke 9:23**; **John 15:2**)—there is *absolutely*, **no** winking at disobedience.

Knowing the Word Trough Obedience

How are we—as the disciples did back then—to **obey** and **keep** His Word? We have an obligation to **know** it—the Spirit will give us its **comprehension**. Jesus taught His own everything in three years, then He entrusted this to His Spirit, to do **the same** for us.

Stifle the Spirit, and His work stalls. Meet His conditions via His Spirit-taught Word, and **John 15:3** holds true for us:

> "You are already **clean because of the Word** which **I have given you** [the **teachings** (His, not someone else's) which **I** (*ibid*) have discussed with **you**]" (**John 15:3**).

So, it's disconcerting then, that if the Holy Spirit is *not teaching us*, how can one then be *absolutely* sure that the above verse applies to us? Only you can answer this, being that this is a personal question between Him and the lector.

One Teacher

God appoints one Person—His Spirit—to **keep us clean** *through His Word*. Scriptures assure me—**no religion needed**, just the same as for those Israelites who **chose** Jesus **over the Pharisees**—we must do this too if we to be clean at **all times**, assuring us, not only for securing our inheritance, but to be ready when He appears to take us home (in the rapture).

Today's sheep are taught by men trained in the human "wisdom" halls—from monasteries to seminaries—echo this to the history of the church, and it explain this 1,800-year drift from the original faith.

Equal in His Eyes

So, what's another flaw in this man operated system? For sure, viewing the sheep as riff-rafts, and lesser than the "holy" Twelve, and the myriads of other "saints," as in the Catholic church. Yet Jesus sent seventy (**Luke 10:1**) with equal powers as the original twelve.

While Protestantism is more subtle about this issue, the Catholic Church amplifies this absurdity, by elevating faithful believers of old, who were living their faith according to His Word, as "saints," far above those sorry pew-sitters—a farce deemed as "sound," but **contrary** to God's Word. With **15 choices** of passages to prove this *religious fallacy* let me choose two, one from each testament:

> "For the Lord delights in justice and does not abandon **His saints** (faithful ones); they are preserved forever, but the descendants of the wicked will [in time] be cut off" (**Psalm 37:28**).

Romans 1:7 echoes it:

"[I am writing] to **all** who are beloved of God in Rome, **called to be <u>saints</u>** (God's people) *and* set apart for a sanctified life, [that is, set apart for God and **His** purpose]."

Yes, the Twelve had an incredible honor walking with Him, but that didn't make them greater or superior, because God sees us as equal, per **Romans 2:11**:

"For God shows **<u>no</u> partiality** [no arbitrary favoritism; with Him one person is **not more important** than another]."

There is no favoritism with God (**Romans 2:11**), and **John 17:20**. He levels the rest of us:

"I do not pray for these alone [it is not for their sake only that I make this request], but also for [**ALL**] those who [will ever] **<u>believe and trust</u>** in Me, through their message."
    (Don't miss above that it is not just "*believing*," but <u>trusting</u>.)

The Cost of Illiteracy

Strangers, Not Friends

The real damage? Sheep taught by men, not the Spirit, remain oblivious to what He is doing, not only in their lives, but all around them—by neglecting His Word **outside** of His personal designated Master Teacher, severs intimate knowledge of Him (**John 15:13-15**)—they remain aloof and disconnected. Think of it as an unbalanced intimate relationship where the fiancée, after pledging an undying love prior to the wedding, she starts to keep the companionship of other boyfriends, **JUST** like Israel did in the O.T. All of a sudden, the woman you love to the point of dying for her, becomes just an acquaintance, not your promised. This situation is poignantly expressed in **2 Cor. 11:2-4**:

"I am jealous for you with a godly jealousy because I have promised you to one husband, to present you as a pure virgin to Christ. But I am afraid that, even as the serpent beguiled Eve by his cunning, your ***minds may be corrupted and led away*** from the **simplicity** of [your sincere and] pure devotion to Christ (**Rev. 2:4**). For [you seem willing to allow it] if one comes and preaches **another Jesus** whom we (our Bible today) have not preached, or if you receive a ***different spirit*** from the one you received, or a different gospel from the one you accepted. You **tolerate** all this beautifully [*welcoming the deception*]."

Reality is that **no one** *can love someone who is an unknown, or a stranger to you* (**John 10:27**; and in **14:15**). Common sense tells us that love demands a deep, personal knowledge and bond.

Churches do **have a role** in the life of a disciple but not peddling nonsense nor in their current form and practices—reform begins with the sheep by **knowing and obeying** His Truth contained in His Word.

The Spirit as Our Only Professor

God gave His Word as our **personal** Textbook, and the Spirit, as our Professor. Sidestepping this, we miss His thoughts, ways, and Word's depth (**Romans 8:26-27; 1 Corinthians 2:11**). The Gospels prove it: Jewish leaders warped Scripture; Jesus, its Author, unveiled it and was rejected by those who should have recognized it, had they known it's real meaning. Daily Spirit-led reading mirrors marriage—intimacy ***grows gradually***, no shortcuts, per **Ephesians 5:31-32**:

"For this reason, a man shall leave his father and his mother (the same as with us ***leaving*** our comfy ***world-centered*** life) and shall ***be joined*** [and be faithfully ***devoted***] to his wife, and the two shall ***become one*** flesh. This mystery [of two becoming one] is great; but I am speaking in **REFERENCE** to [the ***relationship*** of] ***Christ and the church***."

Anyone can gather the history, facts, and information about Him from others (**John 18:34**), but that's **not** the same as knowing Him **<u>personally</u>**.

Facts vs. Fellowship

It is quite obvious and evident throughout His Word that salvation certainly aims as a final destination, what **Ephesians 3:17-18** describes:

> "so that Christ **<u>*may dwell*</u>** in **<u>your</u>** hearts through your faith. And may you, having been [deeply] ***rooted*** and [securely] grounded in **<u>love</u>**, be fully **<u>capable</u>** of **<u>*comprehending*</u>** with all the saints (God's people) the **width** and **length** and **height** and **depth** of His Love [fully **<u>*experiencing*</u>** that amazing, ***endless love***]."

Contrast this to the fact that I know a lot **<u>about</u>** President Trump—but I don't **<u>personally</u>** know him, nor he me. Jesus warns the foolish virgins and religious in **Matthew 25:12**:

"I assure you and most solemnly say to you, I **do not <u>know</u> <u>you</u>** [we have **<u>no</u>** relationship']."

If you don't see how, ***knowing His Word is knowing Him***, you risk being one of the "***called***" but **<u>not</u>** one of the "***chosen***" (**Matthew 22:14**; **Romans 11:7**).

Chapter Five

Being in His Presence is Your Choice

Let's now take a close look at **Matthew 24:22-23** and rather than just letting it go over our head, let analyze what our Lord is **really <u>saying</u> to us** here:

> "For at that time there will be a great tribulation (pressure, distress, oppression), such as has **not occurred** since the **beginning of the world** until now, nor ever will [again]. And if those days [of tribulation] had not been cut short, no human life would be saved; but for the sake of **<u>the elect</u>** (God's **chosen** ones) those days **<u>will be</u> shortened**."

We don't have to labor the point that our Lord is **<u>not referring</u>** to, or addressing the entire multitude of Christians of today, but **<u>only</u>** to those **chosen** found *worthy* (read again **Luke 21:36**) to **<u>escape</u>** *the Tribulation period experience*.

This definitions will clarify it more. The Greek word (*koloboō*) translated as "*shortened*," means—to *dismember (cut off)*—the other Greek word (*eklektos*) translated as "*elect*," means—*chosen* by God *choice*, *select*, i.e., the best of its kind or *class*, excellence preeminent. Any serious student of His Word knows that God often speaks about a "remnant," always in the context of a few, versus the whole of God's people.

Therefore, Jesus' Words about the fact that "*many are called, but few chosen*," makes it clear in what *context* He is saying these words to us.

In **Hosea 4:6**, He identifies **who** the "**many are**," and warned them:

> "My people perish for *lack of knowledge*. You've *rejected My Word*, so I will **reject you** as My priest."

Saved First, Chosen Later

Again, this isn't about *losing salvation*—it is just an **exclusion**, one of **our** *own choice*, from being **chosen** to be a priest before Him, a purely **personal preference** with eternal *consequences*, because, again, entering His Kingdom, is a **privilege**, **not** an **entitlement**.

This right **must be earned** as the passage of **Rev. 22:12-15** and others prove it. Once one understands this, then one can easily understand also, His Words in **Luke 21:36**:

> "But keep *alert at all times* [be **attentive and ready**], praying that you may have the strength and ability [to be **found worthy** and] to *escape* all these things that are going to take place, and **to stand in the presence** (at the Rapture) of the Son of Man [at His coming]."

Similarly, here, we don't have to labor the point that our Lord is describing a *specific time and event* here—the Tribulation happening *milliseconds* after the rapture—nor about the fact that in this passage, He is clearly *warning* those Christians who will be living at that time, that **NOT all** of them are going to be raptured—contrary to the religious philosophy and myth that "*everybody*" has a guaranteed seat and reservation in this Rapture train by just "*believing*". Salvation gives one *only the* **opportunity** *to be chosen* based on our actions.

One Must Be Ready and Watching

Sorry, but *no one* who is **not** *attentive* and **ready**—(**CLEANSED** by His Word [**John 15:3**; **1 John 1:9**; **Rev. 7:13-14**])—to **meet** Him, is **worthy** to *escape* (in the Greek "*to flee* **out of**, *flee away* from), and are *not going to make it*. If anyone can find any wiggle room to interpret His Words otherwise, I would be curious to know how. Anyone is free to totally disagree with this portrayal in His Word and take their chance of being right. Myself? Not a chance to take that risk with eternal consequences!

As noted before, in Exodus, eleven tribes, under the penalty of death, had to camp **outside** the Tabernacle perimeter; only the *Levites alone*, dwelt in the presence of God—foreshadowing **Revelation 22:12-15**'s priestly inner circle **who know His Word**, with **access** to the Tree of Life *and* to **enter** the Heavenly Jerusalem through her Gates.

The Wonder and Miracle of 1 John 1:9

Now, here is the six-million-dollar question: Since none of the gentile church are Levites, **how** do **we** get **into** this exclusive priestly group that will dwell in God's Presence for eternity? **John 13:8**'s foot-washing unveils it, and answers the question:

> "Peter said to Him, 'You will never wash my feet!' Jesus answered, '*Unless* I wash you, you have *no part* [**no FELLOWSHIP**] **with Me** [we can have *nothing* to do with each other]."

Daily Cleansing

We are told that we are cleansed by His Word (**John 15:3**) but **maintaining our purity does matter**. In Eden, God met **all** of Adam and Eve's needs, asking only for their trust—manifested by their **obedience**—and just one rule about the tree in the middle of the Garden. Their disobedience **ended** their **fellowship** with Him, bringing their physical death—but not the life breathed into their spirit (**Gen. 2:7**).

In essence then, the **only** "**sin**"—that is an **offense** against God—that exists, is that of being disobedient to God's commands. We can see then that when Jesus said in **Matt. 12:32**:

> "Whoever speaks a word against the Son of Man will be forgiven; but whoever speaks against the Holy Spirit [by attributing the miracles done by Me to Satan] **will not be forgiven**, either in this age or in the *age* to come" (also in **Mark 3:29**).

This, again, is the **only sin** in play when we *all stand* in front of His Final Judgment Seat—this sin is also a *disobedience* sin, by **not obeying** the gospel message. When we boil down to just one sin, it's easy then to see the absurdity of religions making a catalog of the "big ten," and the itty-bitty little ones that "God winks at." If it wasn't so ridiculous, it might be funny.

A Simple Solution for a Simple Problem

Now, for the religious class being *masters* of the obvious, but *flops* at the *uncomplicated and simplicity* of God's Word to solve man's problems, they proceed to have our Bible dissected and anatomized in seminaries and monasteries, as if it was rocket science, not even realizing that their intellectualization of God's Word is totally useless and *less than zero* by the **spirituality** of His Book.

Therefore, the simplicity of **1 John 1:9**, and **John 13:8-10** is too complicated to solve the **REAL** problem between our God and man and prefer to pursue pure religious fantasies. It's about having the privilege of enjoying **His fellowship** that one must be **purified** (made holy) by **Jesus' blood**, not by "what we do," or of our own righteousness, because He is the ultimate **standard** and **essence** of **Holiness**. And the only way to be **consecrated** to Him, **requires** that we **be holy**, as **He is Holy** (**1Eph. 1:4 1 Peter 1:16, Col. 3:12**), **plus our trust,** and our total **adherence** to Jesus.

Jesus was demonstrating to Peter and the rest (and also to us today), that He is the *only One* who **restores** back that **fellowship** with the Father, when we meet His requisites, because **perfection** is **required** to be before His Presence, due to His **absolute** Holiness

(**Matthew 5:48**; **Deuteronomy 18:13**; **John 17:23**). This solitary sin of **disobedience** is the **only thing** that breaks, like in the Garden of Eden, our communion with Him, but *not the family relationship*, as in the story of the prodigal son (**Isaiah 59:2**; **Leviticus 10:10**; **Ephesians 2:5**).

Perfection's Standards

Jesus, by washing our feet (**all** of our **daily disobedience** sins), **restores** us to the **perfection required** to be in His Presence (in *fellowship* with Him) because of His Holiness.
　Matthew 5:48 demands:

> "Be you therefore **perfect**, even as your heavenly Father **is perfect**."

You see, the average Christian doesn't understand the fundamental **Nature** of God's **absolute and total Holiness**, and this fellowship with Him, *requires and demands* that **we be perfect** as well (His **standard** for having His *companionship with us*)—our fellowship with Him **depends** on this (**Deuteronomy 18:13**; **John 17:23**).
　Although we have been cleansed from **all our past sins** when we first believed the gospel, we must be aware that according to **John 15:3:**

> "the Father is the keeper of **every branch** in Me that *does **not** bear fruit* He takes away,"

therefore, our fruit **MUST** come *from, and **through** Him*, **not from us**. This is *impossible to do* without having His fellowship with us (**John 15:5-6**).
　So, if we don't cleanse ourselves daily by using **1 John 1:9**, *we lose that standard of perfection* because of our daily **disobedience** offenses against Him. It's as simple as that.

Knowing His Book is Knowing His Commands

God has an obvious reason for giving us His Word (the **textbook**) and His Spirit as our personal **Teacher**, to teach us His commands and to *reprimand us* when we break them against His will. By disregarding them, we fall into our own trap. Now the obvious question is, *how are we going to keep* His commandments in His Word, when we are ignorant about them?

Think of the devil as a highway patrolman—once he pulls you over for speeding, you can't plead **ignorance** of the traffic laws and get away from receiving his ticket (punishment in your finances, health, relationships, etc.)—the devil will *take out on you*, his hatred for God because **your actions** puts you under **his authority**, whether you believe it, or like or not.

However, if you have your lawyer riding with you *all the time* (*walking with the Holy Spirit*) He can show him a bond for the **total payment** on the cross for your penalty, then, you're free to go, **no fine**—one of the many privileges of a **John 10:10** life that I have experienced many a times.

We find our bond in **Colossians 2:14**:

> "Having **canceled** the *certificate of debt* consisting of legal demands [that were in force] against us and hostile to us. And this certificate he **completely annulled**, *nailing it to His cross*."

The Gospels show that—Jewish leaders twisted the Scriptures—Jesus, their Author, made it clear to them. Reading His Word **daily** with the Spirit as your Teacher, is like a marriage—intimacy grows over time, without shortcuts, as **Ephesians 5:31-32** says:

> "For this reason, a man shall leave his father and his mother (the world you lived in before Christ) and shall be **joined** (with the Spirit) [and be faithfully devoted] to his wife, and the two **shall become one** flesh. This mystery [of **two becoming one**] is great; but I am speaking with **reference to** [the **relationship** of] Christ and the church."

A Cultural Explanation

When Jesus tried to wash Peter's feet, his gut feeling, due to his strong Jewish roots (see **Acts 10:14** and his words later, to Cornelius), revolted at the sight of Jesus, his Lord, taking the lowest position of a slave in a household, washing the feet of its visitors. This foot-washing job was given to the least skilled slave in a wealthy household and Peter *understood* this.

So, why was this most menial job necessary? Well, in those days' houses did not have indoor plumbing nor showers for obvious reasons, therefore, everyone had to take baths in a public place. However, they had to walk back home and by the time they got there, their feet were dirtied on dusty roads, and the slaves washed them (see **Luke 7:44**)—anyone with unwashed feet (as in **no fellowship** with Him), was **unfit** to enter into a **clean** home.

Peter didn't see the symbolism in our Lord's humble act. However, it does explain **John 13:10** because our Lord was referring to Judas in the *context* of **John 15:3**.

Won't even bother to comment about what the religious people have made out of this humble foot washing act from our Lord, because they have used it to promote a pompous, false, and fake humility among the clergy and the gullible sheep, about something they haven't got a clue about the meaning of it.

Jesus' act was symbolizing the *one act*, that **ensures** our **daily cleansing** to *maintain* our **fellowship** (as He warned Peter) with Him and gave us the key **to be ready** to meet Him in the air (**1 Thess. 4:17**) and **qualify** for our inheritance by practicing **1 John 1:9** at *all times*—refuse to apply it, and fellowship fades, but **not** His family ties with us (as in the prodigal son story).

Confession's Weight

Jesus' humble foot-washing shows how we stay cleansed daily, *moment by moment*. So, let us demystify, *disregarding* the religious myths about "how to walk in the Spirit," by simply following God's command in **1 John 1:9**:

"If we [freely] ___admit___ that we have sinned *and* ___confess our sins___, He is ___faithful and just___ [true to His own nature and promises] and will forgive our ___all___ our sins and ___cleanse us continually___ from ___all___ unrighteousness [our wrongdoing, everything ___not in conformity___ with His will and purpose for us]."

Do not overlook or take lightly the **action** word of "*confessing*" here. The Greek word (*homologeō*) means, "***not to deny***, to confess, i.e. to ___admit___ or *declare oneself* guilty." This is the same, and as serious, as if one is pleading guilty in a court of law, where a judge, or a victim of your crime, is not going *to accept* your remorse, in exchange for reading your mind, but by **your own mouth**. One must follow the pattern of **Matthew 5:24**:

"leave your offering there at the altar and **go** (to the **person you** offended) First make peace with your brother and **then** come and present [to Him] your offering (prayers and supplications)."

Ever wonder why your petitions and requests to God remain unanswered? There is your answer. He will forgive your disobedience of your actions against His will, but He will **not take the place** of the offended party. I won't even bother to comment about the Catholic confessional outright folly.

Sin's Defeat

Doubt this God's sin cleansing model? **Romans 6:1-2** proves it:

"What shall we say [to all this]? Should we **continue in sin** (by **ignoring** this necessary step *to be cleansed* in **1 John 1:9**) and practice sin *as a habit* so that [God's gift of] grace may increase and overflow? Certainly not! How can we, the very ones who **died** to sin, **continue to live** in it any longer?" (considering that He gave *us the* **solution** in this **1 John 1:9** verse).

Romans 8:9-14 adds:

"However, you are not [living] in the flesh [controlled by the sinful nature] but **in the Spirit, if** in *fact* the Spirit of God *lives in you* [**directing** and guiding you]. But if anyone does not have the Spirit of Christ, he ***does not belong*** to Him [and is **not** a child of God]. If Christ lives in you, though your [natural] body is dead because of sin, ***your spirit is alive*** because of righteousness [which **He provides**]. And **_if** the Spirit of Him who raised Jesus from the dead lives in you, He who raised Christ Jesus from the dead will also give life to your mortal bodies through His Spirit, who lives in you. So then, brothers and sisters, ***we have an*** **obligation**, but **not** to our flesh [our human nature, our worldliness, our sinful capacity], **to live** according to the [impulses of the] flesh [our nature **without** the Holy Spirit] for if you are living according to the [impulses of the] flesh, you are going to die. But **if** [you are living] by the [power of the Holy] Spirit **you** (**not** Him) are **habitually** **putting** to **death** the sinful deeds of the body, you **will** [really] ***live forever***. For **all** who are **allowing** *themselves* *to* be **led** by the Spirit of God **are sons** of God."

Please read this passage slowly and methodically, and if you are unable to understand exactly what He is saying to you here, then you need to examine yourself just in the same manner, slowly and methodically. We can ***condense*** the above passage as "should we keep sinning to increase grace? No! How can we, dead to sin, live in it when **1 John 1:9** **frees** us from **living with it?**"

Am I now sinless per **Romans 6:1-2**? No! I'm as sinful as anyone. Must I live with sin? Yes, anyone can but **only if I ignore** 1 John **1:9's** daily cleansing. It's like home garbage—I make it *daily*, but if I don't let it go, I **live** with it—it's *not* the garbage's culpability. It's **all my fault** for *choosing* to *keep living* with it.

The Word's Clarity

Sin's Barrier

His Word explains itself, doesn't it? Sin—anything misaligned with His will—unconfessed per **1 John 1:9**, **blocks** our **fellowship** with Him, but doesn't **cancel** *our salvation*. We're saved, just **the same** as those Egypt's freed slaves. **Revelation 7:14** reveals **why** saints could stand **before** God's Throne:

"These are the people who come **out** of the great tribulation (persecution), and **they** have *washed* their robes and **made them white in the Blood of the Lamb**" (by *applying* **1 John 1:9**).

Unseen Offenses

Early on in my Christian walk I had no idea about any of this wonderful information and therefore, I missed **1 John 1:9**'s role in erasing my daily wrongs—everyday acts like **worrying** over finances, **doubting** my circumstances (family, work), **offending** others, or **dishonoring** human dignity to others that weren't considered "sins" by me—and trust me, the devil made me **pay dearly for my ignorance** to the point that I was practically homeless by the end of 2006. I was left practically without a home, job, savings, and wife.

Why? Well, because all of my actions reflected, unwittingly and unknowingly, a **distrust** in His faithfulness and the integrity of His Word and His promises, which is offensive to Him, and like Job, I placed myself under the authority of His enemy and mine. I had no one to blame but me—I was the one, like Job, who broke that *wall of His protection* between Him and me through fear, self-reliance, and my ignorance about His Word.

Not Using the Most Vital Tool

Most Christians falter here—blind to these sins and never wielding **1 John 1:9** to stay **perfect** before Him. Unwittingly, they drift from His fellowship (**Isaiah 59:2**; **Ephesians 2:1**) and fall right into that place where Satan wants us. One can roll their eyes and chuckle about these reality, but if one really understands the Book of Job, this is the stark spiritual situation of every person that follows our Lord.

What Separates Disciples from "Believers"

In **Numbers 8:14** the Levites—were set apart by their **Word knowledge**—mirroring Spirit-led Christians today through **John 14:26**; and in **16:13**, dwelling near God like them (**Deuteronomy 18:2**; **Joshua 13:14**). By applying **1 John 1:9**, is what restores our joy in our salvation (most of **Psalms**; **Galatians 4:15**, and in **5:22**; **2 Corinthians 1:24**; **Philippians 1:25**)—and sets our eyes in our prize (**1 Corinthians 9:24**; **Colossians 2:18**; **Philippians 3:14**).

Our Inheritance at Stake

Following the Exodus script, the Levites, taught by Moses (a Jesus prototype), symbolize our own spiritual **inheritance** through **Word knowledge** (**Colossians 1:9-10**; **2 Peter 1:2**). Do you see now *what is at stake in this short life* we live here? God wants to give this inheritance to us if we are willing to follow His instructions in our Bible—act on it!

It's most unfortunate that Christians do not even know what they are gambling with their inheritance of entering the Kingdom, by *not* walking in the Spirit, therefore, by never exercising this tool of **1 John 1:9** to keep themselves in Christ's perfection before Him through His Blood, and, in failing to do this, without even *knowing* it, or *wanting to*, they end up separated from Him (*just like the prodigal son*) in a very hostile world without His total protection by living under His wings (**Psalm 36:7**, and in **91:4**; **Matt. 23:37**).

He is quite clear in **Isaiah 59:2** and **Eph. 2:1**, the reason **why** He can't have fellowship with us and in **Hosea 4:6** why we are abdicating our priesthood office, and in the same process we place ourselves under the authority of the god of this world to destroy our financial and health wellbeing, homes and families among many other hardships that you and I have witnessed afflicting most of the church attending Christians.

Salvation Defined

A Wider Lens

If we zoom out and take the 30,000 feet view, one can understand why most Christians live in dire straits, and it's merely because they are **not walking in** (see **Deut. 5:33; Micah 6:8**), **fellowship** with Him, being taught in their own chosen religious teachers, who like them, don't yet understand, or know about, this amazing tool to **stay perfect before Him**.

There is a lot more to this, but we'll leave it at that for you and the Spirit, to sort it all out.

The Levites' Distinction

Why were the Levites chosen by God over the eleven other tribes? We can only guess but Moses and Aaron the instruments of the Exodus feat and accomplishment may have played a role in their election—we cannot also overlook that they alone knew God's Word via Moses' teaching—a Jesus' prototype, and Aaron his voice—the same role of the Holy Spirit for the saints. This calling—once open only to one tribe—is now **open to all** of the saints (**2 Peter 1:10; 2 Thessalonians 1:11**). Why? I believe that **John 8:35-36** may answer that for us:

> "Now the **slave does not remain** in a household forever; the Son [of the master] does remain forever. So, if the Son **makes you free**, then you are **unquestionably** free."

All are free to use that freedom to **truly know** the Word of God where we find the keys for everyone to find the opportunity how to transcend, *from slavery to sonship*.

Religion's Blindness

This is just one example of the extent of the damage inflicted to the sheep by the religious establishment making them as blind as themselves (**Matt. 15:14**). This gave the devil a free hand to take away this *spiritual mean* of drawing us **closer to Jesus** as His disciples, where:

> "We **do not** become discouraged [spiritless, disappointed, or afraid]. Though our outer self is [**progressively**] wasting away, yet our **inner self** is being [**progressively**] renewed day by day" (**2 Cor. 4:16**).

Religion blinds the sheep (**Matthew 15:14**), robbing intimacy with Jesus as **disciples**, not as mere "**believers.**"

Exodus was written for us (**Romans 15:4; 1 Corinthians 10:6**), to mirror God's **Hosea 4:6** warning as to whether **we want to be** His **priests**, or merely the Kingdom's subjects. **Matthew 22:13-14** cautions us about this choice:

> "Then the King said to the attendants, 'Tie him (the *lazy servant*) hand and foot and throw him into the *darkness outside* (as *compared* to the Light of His Presence); in that place there will be weeping [over sorrow and pain] and grinding of teeth [over distress and anger].' For *many* are called (*invited, summoned*), but *few* are *chosen.*"

The Greek word "*Called*" used here, means "*invited*" to (as in a banquet but found **unfit** to be at the banquet place)—not in the context of him not *being saved*.

Priesthood Open for All

In **Numbers 8:14** the Levites (**one** tribe out of 12) symbolize the New Testament saints **who willfully choose** His priesthood—all (Levites) were called to be priests (**Romans 15:16; 1 Peter 2:9; Revelation 5:10**) but now, through God's **impartiality** to His Church (**Deuteronomy 10:17; Romans 2:11**), *He offers it* **to all** *us*, **as a choice**—unlike the Levites by their lineage. Will we seize it and be one of the **chosen** out of the many **called**? Only you can decide that for yourself.

Obedience's Reward

Now that we have identified the reason for the Christian religion's problem, and the total failure to the sheep by the enforcers of the current religious establishment system, what's the benefit of our obedience should we act to these disclosures from God's Word?

Well, for me, now that I am *experiencing* the sure promise of **Psalms 127:1, Zech. 4:6,** and **John 10:10** in my personal and spiritual walk with Him, is that I can enjoy, unlike my previous church experiences, a stress-free relationship with Him while having full access to **all** of His available resources revealed in His Word—the biggest one of them all, found in **Zechariah 4:6** that tells us:

> "Then he said to me, 'This [*continuous supply of oil* (His Spirit)] is the **Word of the Lord** to Zerubbabel [prince of Judah], saying, *not by might*, nor *by power*, but **by My Spirit** [of whom *the oil is a symbol*],' says the Lord of hosts."

Church Reimagined

Now, regarding the role of a local church. Pastors **must submit** to God's design and order, humbling themselves to His Spirit, and individually help **each sheep** sent to him to grow and multiply. This takes time and patience, and it depends on both, pastor and sheep **obeying** the voice of the Spirit. Each sheep needs personal guidance in their study of the Word—not as a *"professor,"* but as an *assistant counselor* to God's Spirit. Pastors must focus on those who *diligently seek* God's Spirit and His will.

These sheep would not be difficult to recognize and assist among the flock, in amplifying their spiritual development in due time through the pastor's broader and extensive experience with His Word. However, if the pastor is *not walking in the Spirit*, whatever he does will be just another human religious program doomed to certain failure.

Pastors' Role Retested

If someone still doubts that pastors are not to be teachers, dispute this: if **Ephesians 4:11** assigns pastors as God's teachers, then **1 Corinthians 12:5-11** should list it among the listed Spirit-given ministries. Check it: wisdom, knowledge, faith, healing, miracles, prophecy, discernment, tongues, interpretation—all Spirit-driven, no "pastors" included here. Teaching God's Word **is a spiritual**, **job** per **1 Corinthians 2:11**:

> "So, **NO ONE knows** *the things of God* **Except** the Spirit of God."

Equipping, Not Teaching

It's easy, then, to logically conclude that **not one person**—whether it be you, me, or the person of religion one follows—is **capable of operating** at this spiritual level—then, no matter how sincere he or she is, **every** human effort to do this their own way, will **fall short** of God's intended results.

Now let's look at **Ephesians 4:11-14** in its **entire** context:

> "And [His gifts (not ministry) to the church were varied and] He *Himself appointed* some as apostles [special messengers, representatives], some as prophets [who speak a new message from God to the people], some as evangelists [who spread the good news of salvation], and some as *pastors* and **instructors** (as meant in the original Greek language) [to *shepherd*, *guide*, and *instruct*], [and He did this] to **fully equip** and *perfect* the saints (God's people) for **works of service**, to *build up* the body of Christ [the Church]; until we *all reach* **oneness** *in the faith* (never seen since the third century) and in the **knowledge** of the Son of God, [growing spiritually] to become a perfect man (erroneously translated as "*believers*" in some translations), reaching to the [highest] measure of the fullness of Christ [man-

ifesting His spiritual completeness and **exercising our** (*not* your pastor or *any* other religious figure) spiritual gifts in unity]. So that **we** are *no longer children* [spiritually **immature**], tossed back and forth [like ships on a stormy sea] and *carried about* by every wind of [shifting religious] **doctrine**, by the cunning and trickery of [unscrupulous] men, by the deceitful scheming of people ready to do anything [for personal **profit**]."

If this passage does not describe this world's current religious establishment, I don't know what other depiction would be.

It's All Up to Us Not Him

Obviously, what the reader does with all of this information being spelled out here, God leaves that choice entirely up to us, because God always respect our free will and *final* say (no pun intended). This passage above indicts today's religious chaos—pastors are to guide, not teach, as that is in the Spirit's domain.

Pastors' Function

Is there another witness scripture to establish that the office of pastoring a congregation **does not** include teaching as a ministry and appointed work? Yes, there is.

If a pastor, or priest were supposed to teach a congregation, then **1 Peter 5:1-2** would be the *perfect, if not ideal* passage to confirm and stipulate this, that pastors do have such teaching ministry, but does it? No! It confirms *exactly* what **Eph. 4:11-2** says. Let's read it:

"I strongly urge the elders among you [*pastors, spiritual leaders* of the church], as a fellow elder and as an eyewitness [called to testify] of the sufferings of Christ, as well as one who shares in the glory that is to be revealed: **shepherd** and **guide**, and **protect** *the flock of God* among you, exercising **oversight** not under compulsion, but voluntarily, **according to the will** of God."

Does anyone see anywhere here that says that they are to be the "*theologians*" for expounding God's Word to the flock? I certainly *do not* see that at all.

No "*theologist*" mandate here—*guidance*, not exposition.

Words Redefined by Its Greek Roots

"Teachers" (**Ephesians 4:11**) isn't about being a "**theologizer**"—in both, the Greek, and the Hebrew, it means "to *guide*, *lead*, *tutor* the *uninformed*, *inexperienced*, and even the illiterate." "**Pastor**" means to *coach*—"*chasten*, *unite*"—and not to usurp the Spirit's teaching role, and **1 Corinthians 12:4-11** omits pastoring as an *appointed ministry* by the Spirit. They are to guard the truth of His Word, **mentoring** new converts, and cheerlead—complementing a Spirit-led study *by the sheep*.

Holy Calling

They are also called to complement the flock in their **own studies** and in their walk with our Lord, illuminating their path towards understanding the One who called them, so that we all can **grasp and know** why:

> "He delivered us and saved us and *called us with a holy calling* [a calling that leads to a *consecrated life*—a life *set apart*—a life *of purpose*], not because of our works [or because of any personal merit—we could do nothing to earn this], but because of His own purpose and grace [His amazing, undeserved favor] which was granted to us in Christ Jesus before the world began [eternal ages ago]" (**2 Timothy 1:9**).

The Real Jesus

Beyond Manmade Façades

Let's shed off the tired labels—Catholic, Mormon, Protestant, Baptist, and more—each of them crafting a "Jesus" out of their own imagination and denominational manmade creeds and beliefs. These groups peddle their version like salespeople hawking wares, focusing on how to raise donations over preaching the truth by knowing how to tickle the congregation's ears (**2 Tim. 4:3**). **No pastor or preacher** can **replicate** the Holy Spirit's work, as God designed it. Discipleship is a calling—personal and voluntary—like the Twelve apostles, and free to decline the call of **Colossians 1:10**:

> "**Walk** in a manner ***worthy*** of the Lord [displaying admirable character, moral courage, and personal integrity], to [fully] ***please*** Him in ***all*** things, **bearing *fruit*** in every good work and ***steadily growing*** in the **KNOWLEDGE** of God [with deeper faith, clearer insight and fervent love for ***His precepts*** (in His Word]."

A Father's Wish

Our Father mirrors an earthly parent's longing for closeness with a child—needing time to grasp their hopes. Knowing **our Father** as Jesus did defies words—and is unique to each sheep, experientially just like siblings in a family. Once I reached this, I'd never will revert to religion's sterile shell I experienced when I first come to Him. Remarkably, this shift from the rut of practicing a religion wasn't self-driven, but God's grace of opening my spiritual ears and eyes when I longed for something better, and not knowing whether I had a chance to build my own spiritual house, per **Psalm 127:1**:

> "**Unless** the Lord **builds** the house, they labor ***in vain*** who build it; unless the Lord guards the city, the watchman keeps awake ***in vain***."

Religion's Futility

For thirty-five years, I built my spiritual house on a religious foundation and the flesh—fruitless, devoid of peace and security in my family, finances, and health. I don't fault churches—they followed their training, as did I, with other blind sheep in tandem. Yet God turned it for good (**Romans 8:28**). No more intermediaries—seeking to know God from others rather than from Himself—it's like needing a neighbor, or friend to stand and mediate between me, and my parents, and explain to me who they are, and what they think, when all along, I am the one knowing and living with them—it's insane!

Why then, should God's children allow someone else to stand as a mediator between their Heavenly Father and them? Didn't He **clarify whose role** is that, in **1 Tim. 1:5**:

> "For there is [only] one God, and [only] **ONE Mediator** between God and mankind, the Man Christ Jesus" (also in **Hebrews 8:6**; and in **9:15** and **12:24**).

Knowing vs. Believing

Believing in a religious "something" pales against knowing Him personally. Seeking a discipleship—is where the fullness in the Godhead is found (**Colossians 2:8-10**)—which **demands** only His Spirit's work, not from us, or from others. Once you obey His commands, it is then when one is able to grasp **1 Corinthians 2:12-15** that we:

> "Have **NOT** **received** the spirit of the world (so common in our religious circles), but the Spirit who is **FROM** God (Not some religion, denomination, or preacher), so that we may **KNOW** the things freely given to us *BY* God (Ibid). We also speak these things, *NOT* in words taught by human wisdom, but in those taught *BY* the Spirit, combining spiritual thoughts with spiritual words. But a natural person does not accept the things of the Spirit of God, for they are foolishness to him; and he *cannot understand* them, because they are spiritually *DISCERNED*.

But the one, who is spiritual, discerns _**all**_ things, yet he himself, is judged by **_NO ONE_**" (**1 Cor. 2:12-15**).

God's Word Insights Come Only from the Spirit

The facts are that men **cannot discern** or teach His Word's depth—**only** His Spirit can (**1 Corinthians 2:11**):

> "**NO ONE** _**knows**_ the **thoughts** of God, **_EXCEPT_** the _Spirit of God._"

He truly **IS** the **NARROW** Door that we **MUST** enter in, nevertheless, a lot of the Christians choose other entrances, _**despite**_ of His Word in **John 10:7-9**:

> "Jesus said to them again, 'Truly, truly I say to you, I am **THE DOOR** of the sheep. **ALL** (**not** some or most, or one who is "special," or unique) those who came before Me (religious men) are thieves and robbers, but the (**real**) sheep _**did not LISTEN**_ to them (the religious establishment). I am the door; if anyone **enters TROUGH** Me (**NOT** a religion and their "shepherds"), he **WILL** be saved."

Personally, I don't think that He is using hyperbole here but clearly saying that there is only **ONE RIGHT** way to enter the Kingdom, and it's **not** _through a church door._ He doubles-down later in **John 10:27-28**:

> "The sheep that are My **own** (not those in some denomination or religion), **hear** _My voice and listen to Me_ (again, not someone else's); I **know** them, and they follow **Me**. And **I** (Ibid) give them eternal life, and they will **never, ever** [by any means] perish; and no one will ever snatch them out of My hand."

Chapter Six

The Peril of Losing
Our Inheritance

The Religious Presumption

It may be that these truths will clash with religious norms—where the idea of God's having intimacy with "their own personally owned denominational sheep," instead of Jesus,' is not in their religious playing cards, nor in their narrative. Never mind that He **created us** for **this inheritance**—this our purpose for living our life in this planet. Many *will trade it* for the worldly trinkets of materialism, power, fleeting pleasures, money's false joy, and the rest.

I've tasted it all—they proved it to be as hollow as a soda straw. Reject His way, and you're in dire danger of being one the billions "*called*," but **not** one of the few "*chosen*" (**Matthew 22:14; John 15:16; 1 Peter 2:9**), forfeiting your priesthood forever—a failing that is inherent and natural in church building environment and will remain so, I am sure, until His Second coming.

Spiritual Abuse

This Word illiteracy—manipulating Christian's emotions while sitting in pews waiting for a feel-good show—mirrors the era of Judges after Johsua and his generation passed on. What the religious organizations have achieved is no different than someone taking a jet liner and deciding to use it as a transportation bus on a highway—both move, but one soars. Regardless, only one is designed to be the absolute best to deliver someone from point A to point B, during a lifetime.

I know that what we have discussed here so far is highly uncomfortable, controversial, provocative, debatable, and certainly, one big matza ball in the throat of any religious minded person out there, and definitely, will be extremely hard to swallow. The Pharisees and Sadducees of His time proved this to be absolutely true. Nevertheless, these principles and truths that I am presenting here, are not about what I "think, believe, or have made up," but merely reading what has been written in His Word in plain Hebrew and Greek, translated into simple English.

Hopefully, it will be a challenge to some—being that is backed by biblical evidence, to anyone else who is **seeking the Truth**, and want to find it out **for themselves**, about what He has already **declared in His Word**, and even better, a reliable yardstick to **measure one's progress in the faith**, as compared to the experiences one gets at any one of the choices of religions that exist out there today.

Rediscovering Love

If anything, this information is just a chance to do your own research and own homework about the precision, and clarity of His written Word, and the opportunity to be thrilled once more, and I mean truly ecstatic and excited, by reacquainting oneself with Him again. He is the only One who is capable of changing your entire life in the here, and now, and to guarantee the place you were meant to have in eternity. But, even more than that, a new opportunity of falling in love with Him, all over again, as when we first met Him. Needless to say, there is no comparison, or resemblance, with any of my early experiences I had in the religious world, or in those daily, week in, and week out external works to prove to myself, that I was really "living the real Christian" life.

Get to research this for yourself, His Word's accuracy, and simplicity—reacquaint yourself, fall in love anew. No resemblance to religion's rote works.

This religious life results in what **Revelation 2:4** accuses us of:

"But I have this [charge] *against* you, that you have **left** your *first love* [you have lost the *depth* of love that you *first had for Me*]."

Seeking Heartfully

I can personally testify to all my readers that, after supernaturally experiencing His Love that night of my salvation, back in August 1975 where, in just the span of a few years, this charge against me was true in my life. The commitment I had made to Him that evening, proved to be shallow, and the "faith" that I "thought" I had, was actually manufactured by myself. After that day, going to church had become no more than having another social engagement, rather than being in a golf course, or the neighborhood bar, neither one being of consequence, nor depth.

In my life, it was merely a comforting "feel good" requirement that remained, as it were, a quixotic dream, collecting dust on my mental fantasy shelves—disguising faith as hope and wishing and waiting for the day in which I would die to experience them. We wander in spiritual halls cloaking uneasy and distressing feelings as counterfeit joy—never satisfying, nor bringing real peace. He didn't craft this shift in my life—I did it all by myself. But once I obeyed **Deuteronomy 4:29**, everything began to change:

"Seek the Lord your God, and you **will find** Him **IF** you search for Him with **all** your heart and all your soul" (also in **1 Chronicles 28:9**, **Jer. 29:13** and others).

Again, if this huge matza ball concept happens to be just as big for anyone else, as it was for the Pharisees and the Sadducees as mentioned before, then the problem is **not** with the message delivered, but because of religious obstacles of *unbelief*, *stiffness*, and *inflexi-*

bility that it is still with us today as well. They had closed their minds about the possibility that God's:

> "Thoughts are **not your thoughts**, nor are **your ways** My ways, declares the Lord. 'For as the heavens are higher than the earth, so are My ways **higher** than your ways, and My thoughts higher than your thoughts' " (**Isaiah 58:8-9**).

Challenging the Old

A New Way

And for these Jews, it was all because what Jesus had presented to them the truth that was something **different** than their own religious ideas and ways that they had been *indoctrinated* with, and *drilled* into their minds, which challenged centuries of old religion conditioning that their religious establishment had been circulating for the previous 1,500 years, and for us today, for at least 1800 years. No wonder His frustration shines through in the book of John at their national blindness, as illustrated in the fact that there were only 120 disciples at Pentecost. **Luke 13:24** warns:

> "Strive to **enter** through the ***narrow door*** [*force* aside ***unbelief*** and the attractions of sin]; for many, I tell you, will try to enter [by **their own** (religious) works] and ***will not*** be able."

And in **John 8:43**:

> "Why do you ***misunderstand*** what I am saying? It is because [your ***spiritual ears are deaf*** and] you are ***unable to hear*** [the **truth** of] **My Word**."

Then, later, in **Hebrews 3:19**, He tells the N.T. saints why **Christians**, like the saved Jews out of Egypt, are in *danger* of also losing their inheritance:

"So, we see that they (the Jewish slaves) were *not able to enter* [*into* His rest—the promised land (like Christians today)] *because* of **unbelief** and an **unwillingness** to **trust** in God (Words)."

Blind Acceptance

Actually, all things being equal, it's not the churches' fault—they teach as trained. It is actually the fact, that the faithful swallow it all as "gospel truth," like the Jews under their rabbis, *assuming that their traditions* are God's Word. Responsibility rests on us for accepting all of these errors **without questioning** them. But this is to be expected since religion, whatever it might be, is part of all cultures, *no differently* than art, music, or folklore dances.

So, if one doesn't know what rights **God gives** to those who **answer** *His call*, how would you then fight back against those spiritual entities that **rule** *this world* through their own established human institutions? It's no different than someone being falsely arrested and, if he/she *does not know* their rights under the Constitution of their country, how is one to defend oneself?

Heartfelt Reaction

The Samaritan woman received the necessary information from our Lord, to correct her beliefs ever since the days of Jeroboam, and she took His Word **seriously**, and even better, **acted** on it. However, unlike us today, this Samaritan woman had a *valid excuse* of not knowing God's will, due to her ignorance about God's true Word at that time, since no one could read, nor afford parchments except the religious ruling class and the wealthy. Nevertheless, after our Lord revealed the Truth to her, had she not acted on it, that excuse would evaporate once she *knew* about it *firsthand*, from the author of the Word. So, with all of the tools He has given us today, what's our excuse?

He encourages us in **Colossians 3:23-24** to:

"**Whatever** you do [whatsoever *your* task it may be], work from the soul [that is, put in your very best effort (He is *not* looking for perfection in us)], as [something done] for the Lord and not **for** men, *knowing* [with all *certainty*] that it is *from* the Lord [*not* from men] that you **will receive** the **inheritance** which is **your** [**greatest**] reward" (see **2 Timothy 3:13-14**; and **2 Peter 3:17**).

Now, if anyone thinks that by just "***believing***" is their free get-out jail card from the ***responsibility*** of **acting** on His Word and get an inheritance—sorry—His Word makes it clear here that **it is not so**, it's **our response after knowing His Words** that will determine our inheritance.

In **Matt. 7:24-27**, He warns us about the ***two foundations*** one can build on, and identifies which one is the successful one if you make the right choice:

"So, everyone who **hears** these Words of Mine and **acts** on them, will be like a wise man [a far-sighted, practical, and sensible man] who built his house on the rock. And the rain fell, and the floods *and* torrents came, and the winds blew and slammed against that house; yet it did not fall, because it had been founded on the **rock**. And **everyone** who hears these words of Mine and **does not** do them, will be like a foolish (stupid) man who built his house on the sand. And the rain fell, and the floods *and* torrents came, and the winds blew and slammed against that house; and it fell—and great and **complete** was its fall" (as affirmed in **1 Cor. 3:11-15**).

None of this is about our salvation, but it's about our potential ***life's quality in this life*** (**John 10:10**) and a future inheritance that hinges on our **obedience**, to His Word and using **1 John 1:9** to *stay clean and ready to meet Him*, and for *maintaining* a **24/7** fellowship with Him.

Accountability's Weight

If one cannot understand any this, then one cannot apprehend such mystery verses that we find all over the Gospels, such as this one in **Luke 12:47-49**:

> "And that servant who **knew** his master's **will**, and yet *did not get ready* or **act** in *accord* with His will, will be beaten with many lashes [of the whip], but the one who *did not know* it and did things worthy of a beating, will receive only a few [lashes]. From **everyone** to whom much has been given, much will be **required**; and to whom they entrusted much, of him they will ask all the more."

True Worship

When the Spirit explains His Word (**1 Corinthians 2:11**), there are *no* mysteries—only for those who prefer to remain uninformed and misinformed. Pastors are supposed to guide and train disciples to build up the church (**Ephesians 4:11**). But the reality is, that they have only *produced* "**believers**," not **disciples** so, by His standards, today's "church" has not only failed miserably on this, but also that they have *missed* entirely the **meaning** behind the words in **John 4:21-24's** **topic** and its truth behind it.

So, let's revisit the Samaritan woman's exchange with our Lord:

> "Jesus replied, 'Woman, **believe** Me, a time is coming [when God's salvation comes] when **you** (individually) will worship the Father *NEITHER* on this mountain, nor in Jerusalem (or your church). **You** (and many of us today) **do not know** what you worship; we [Jews] do know what we worship, for salvation is from the Jews. But time is coming, and it is **ALREADY here** when the **TRUE** worshipers **will** worship the Father **in SPIRIT** [from the heart, the inner self, (impossible without His Spirit)] and in **truth** (in our Bible); for the Father **seeks** such people to **be** His worshipers. God is Spirit [the Source of life, yet invisible to mankind], and those who worship Him **MUST** worship (**no**

other *choice* given here) in **SPIRIT** (inside us) and **truth**' (our Bibles, if we choose to read and study it)."

It doesn't take a genius then that we can *rephrase* our Lord's Words to this woman as:

"Woman, **believe** Me, a time is coming when **you** (individually) will worship the Father *NEITHER* at the catholic, protestant, Mormon, etc. church, **NOR** in Mecca, Tibet, India, etc."

Many believers chase religion's superficial appeal, *crafting a God they personally like*, blind to His will in Scripture. All of this it's simple to understand for the Spirit led—but rocket science only to the religious institutions.

Salvation's Core

Consider salvation's common spin coming from pulpits that I have *personally* heard: "Confess your sins, be *born again*—that's the key." Partly true—but that is only some of its steps, **not** the whole process. **Romans 10:9-10** clarifies it:

"If you **CONFESS** with your mouth **JESUS** as **Lord** (of *your* life, **NOT** sins), and **believe** in *your heart* (*not* with your *mind*) that God raised Him from the dead, *you* **WILL** be *saved*; for with the **heart** (again, **not** the mind as common in our churches out of **fear**, or by the **selling** of a denomination or a religion) a person *believes*, **resulting** in righteousness, and with the mouth he *confesses*, **RESULTING** in salvation"
(This is **confirmed** in **Matt. 10:32, Luke 12:8** [Jesus confessing us as saved], and in **Acts 16:31**, and **Rom. 1:16**).

Confession Unpacked

Believing with the heart is another personal issue that is between the Lord and His sheep, so, let's take that out of the equation. Let's examine then the word *"confess,"* in the original language to understand better what this passage is saying:

"**Confess**" (Greek *homologeō*): means "to *agree, declare openly*"—not just sins, but Jesus' Lordship **over your life**. Again, this is a heart issue, between sheep and Lord—no middleman needed.

"**Confess**," then, in the above passage, simply means to declare one's guilt, and accepting the death sentence for the **sin** of not agreeing with the Spirit's message about the gospel in your mind and heart. By this assent, one then accepts Jesus to be our **substitute** on that cross (**Romans 1:16**).

Once this **belief** is set in stone in your heart and mind (believing what you *know is true* in your heart), then confessing the sin of *making yourself your own god*, is what **brings** **salvation**. After salvation, the goal is to become a **disciple** not just an **unproductive** "*believer*."

The other goal is that one **must remain clean** from daily sins that *we are bound to commit*, no matter who you are, since **all** the sins of your past are already blotted out for eternity by just **obeying 1 John 1:9**:

> "If we [freely] ***admit*** that we have sinned *and **confess our sins**,* He is ***faithful and just*** [true to His own nature and promises] and will forgive our ***all*** our sins and ***cleanse us continually*** from ***all*** unrighteousness [our wrongdoing, everything ***not in*** conformity with His **will** and **purpose** for us]."

Staying on the Vine

Let's review how to train our minds to consistently use **1 John 1:9** in our daily life. and *avoiding* the Father's pruning (**John 15:2-3**) us *off the Vine* and losing a constant fellowship with our Savior and thus, **not producing** any **fruit supplied by Him**, and *Him alone*, and not by us with our religious works, but rather, *through* our **obedience** to His Word (**Matthew 7:24-27**), just like it was in the wilderness for the Jewish slaves **after being saved** out of Egypt!

Past Sins are Forgiven Forever

In my personal opinion, the average Christian (I being one for decades) haven't been *taught* that when we come to Him for our salvation, **ALL**, **100%** *of our sins*—from the age of accountability to that moment—once we invite Him into our heart, have been forever forgiven, just as He promises us in **Psalm 103:11-12**, quoted before.

Hebrews 10:14 affirms this truth:

> " For by the one offering, He has **perfected <u>forever</u>** *and* **completely <u>cleansed</u>** (from our sins) those who are being sanctified [*bringing each believer to spiritual* <u>completion</u> *and* <u>maturity</u>]."

Post-salvation, only our daily sins need confessing—the unbelief (as in the wilderness) **offends** God (**Hebrews 3:19**; and in **4:6**). If one chooses to ignore **1 John 1:9** one risks constant **separation** from Him.

One **must** come to recognize that God is *sensitive* about **our** (like the slaves) **<u>doubting</u>** His promises, and by our **<u>unbelief</u>**, as clearly shown in the Exodus story (also in the **Book of Hebrews**) where this kind of attitude, *innocent or not*, **<u>will bring</u>** into play **Hebrews 3:19**, and **4:6** into play, in *your* daily life, *unintended* and with *unpleasant* consequences—a courtesy from your friendly devil's associates running around in your neighborhood and in every church of your choice.

Therefore, one *cannot afford*, nor allow any unwanted separation from His fellowship between us and Him, by ignoring and not applying **1 John 1:9** every second of our life, if necessary. Christians tend to forget the half million plus slaves died after leaving Egypt *never reaching* the Promised Land.

Psalm 103:11-12 confirms the finality of God's forgiveness of sins:

> "For as the heavens are high above the earth, so great is His lovingkindness toward those who fear and worship Him [with awe-filled respect and deepest reverence]. As **<u>far</u>** as the *east is*

from the west, so far has He **removed** our transgressions from us" (also in **Ephe. 1:7**; **Col. 1:14**).

Post-Salvation Living

Daily Cleansing

At the risk of redundancy—but that's what makes jetliners safe—in our post-salvation status, we only need to **confess** our **daily** sin-breaking fellowship, as Jesus warned Peter in **John 13:8, so,** let's climb that mountain again:

> "Unless **I** wash **you** (not your church confessional or other hocus pocus religious solutions), you have **no part** [**no fellowship**] with Me'."

Like a dirty car, an impure spiritual life, driven by living in fear, doubt, anger, and envy, etc., ***without solving*** the problems in your life—**offends** God's faithfulness to *fulfill every promise* that He has made *personally* to **you** (**Hebrews 3:12-16**; **1 John 1:9**). Doubting His ability to accomplish His purpose for your life is an ***affront*** to Him and **severs** your fellowship with Him and puts a **separation wall** (**Isaiah 59:2**; **Deut. 27:26**), between Him and you, cutting off fellowship, and a constant communion with Him. This is the kind of lessons found all over the story of Exodus but, due to poor instruction, Christians are blind to them.

Abundant Life Unlocked

Focusing away from this offense of unbelief and de-facto self-enforced mistrust, and choosing instead to concentrate on our **daily relationship** with Him, which certainly will unlock, for **any obedient** child of His, the promised abundant life of **John 10:10**. And please, don't think this some prosperity message nonsense, but fulfilling His promise in **Matt. 6:33**, where—I am a firsthand witness that—He has met **every single need**, *not my wants*, that I have ever had for the last umpteen years.

Nothing more, nothing less. Hard? Not really—just that we have to:

> "Continue to **work out** your [own] salvation [that is, cultivate it, bring it to full effect, actively pursue spiritual maturity] with awe-inspired fear and trembling [using serious caution and critical self-evaluation to **avoid** anything that might offend God or discredit the name of Christ]" (**Phil. 2:12**).

Commitment's Test

In my experience, as I focused on staying close to Him every moment of my life, it was then when I began, little by little, to start living the life of **John 10:10** that He has promised to **each one of us**. Can anyone do this on a consistent basis? Yes, but it requires **real** *commitment*, *dedication*, and *steadfastness* from the heart, and persevering in every difficult moment in our daily lives. Believe me, this will be put to the test when dealing with other human beings (our neighbor in **Matt. 5:24**; **Luke 10:29**) regardless of whether they are part of our family, or a total stranger. However, these changes in your life all begin by actively **obeying Matt. 6:33**, which counsels us to:

"But *first* and *most importantly* **seek** (aim at, strive after) His kingdom and His righteousness [*His* **way** *of* **doing** *and being* **right**—*the* **attitude** *and* **character** *of God*], and **all** these things (your physical, mental, and financial needs, **not wishes**) **will** be **given** to you also."

The Born-Again Ruse

Salvation is Not a Synonym with Being Born Again

Despite the devil's cunning dogma since *the invention of the Christian religion* in the third century, namely that salvation is *equivalent to being born again*—sorry no, **it is not**!—this demonic doctrine (**1 Timothy 4:1**) confuses the **difference** between being just *saved*, *born again*, and *entering the Kingdom*.

Salvation **does lead** to a communion with God, **if ALL of His conditions are met**, as we have been discussed throughout here, and, not to mention, *not constantly offending* Him (like the slaves in the desert did)—they are **distinct from each other**. It is like water—one molecule of hydrogen (the soul), one molecule of oxygen (the human spirit)—they have *two different natures*, just as these two gases are.

However, by themselves, they **lack eternal life** (**Ephesians 2:1**; and in **2:5, Colossians 2:13**). He himself gives us the **definition of how to acquire** eternal life in **John 17:3**:

> "And **THIS IS eternal life**, that they may **KNOW You**, the only true God, **and Jesus Christ**, whom you have sent."

Please tell me, where do you see, or find here, whereby just by "*believing*," gives *anyone* eternal life? As stated before, these religious folks also believe that salvation and entering the Kingdom are also the same.

It's Our Living Water

Let's use human terms—the process it's similar to the configuration of water—**Salvation** is one molecule of hydrogen, and being **born again** is the other hydrogen molecule. However, to make it *living water* (the **Word of God through** His Spirit), the source of all life, **requires a molecule** of oxygen.

So, where do we get this third *molecule*? Yes, it's quite obvious—the **Spirit of God** is that molecule of oxygen that, when *combined* with our salvation and new birth, produces life-giving water—this is what **guarantees our entry** into the Kingdom of God.

At first glance, this statement seems, especially to the indoctrinated religious mind, as an "attack on their religious beliefs and traditions," which are based on accepting erroneous teachings *as if they were based on the Word of God*.

These dogmas, including the idea that every Christian is a "*child of God*," have been drilled and instilled for centuries. And no,

Paul used this phrase with the Athenians just to get their attention, but he didn't validate it as truth. Nevertheless, this *disparity* between **salvation**, being **born again**, and **entering the Kingdom** is easily understood by reflecting on the composition and combination of the water molecules, as mentioned above.

So, returning to the **basic composition** of our **total salvation** and each state of its being, the new question is—can we expect any **equivalence in the nature** of these three Christian growth developments, which are separate and individual states in the growth of the Christian life?

No! They are **independent** of each other until, like water, they are combined.

That is **the difference** between *being saved from the wrath of God*, being *born again* from **above**, and *entering the Kingdom*. All of them **must be** combined for us **to be a priest** before our God according to **Hosea 4:6** requirement.

Born Again Defined

Let's now refute this religious devious and deceptive doctrinal error, sowed by God's enemy, with tremendous success I might add, into the minds of the Bible illiterates cluttering the aisles of the religious establishment churches.

The word *born again* appears only **four times** in the New Testament, in **John 3:3**; and **3:7**, (as defined in **1:13**), and in **1 Peter 1:3** and in **1:23**, where, in **John's Book**, the context of the text **clearly** indicates that *born again*, is merely the **REQUIREMENT** to open our **own** *spiritual eyes* (but only true **if** your spirit is **united** with His Spirit).

It is only then, that one can "**see** and **experience**" the Kingdom of God as explained by Him in **John 3:3** below.

Now, **1 Peter 1:3**, is just *confirming* **John 3:3-7**, and is about the **two natures**, or composition, of human beings today, one *eternal* (his spirit) and the other *temporal* (the body). We seem to forget that the state of being born again actually means, "**reborn from above—not from below** by a religion—is about being **spiritually** *"transformed, renewed,* and *sanctified"*—something that **ONLY** **His Spirit can do**—and not by anything we do, say, or perform **for any** religious group or denomination.

Let's *confirm* this as **defined** by Christ Himself, in **John 3:3**:

"I assure you and most solemnly say to you, unless a person is born again [reborn **from above**—spiritually **transformed, renewed, sanctified**], he **cannot** [**ever**] **see** and **experience** the Kingdom of God."

And in the following verses in **3:6-7**:

"That which is born of the flesh *is flesh* [the physical is merely physical], and that which is born of the Spirit *is spirit.*(His Spirit united with your spirit). Do not be surprised that I have told you, 'You **must** be **born again** [reborn **from above**]— [**spiritually transformed, renewed, sanctified**']."

So, in **1 Peter 1:23** again, confirms **John 3:3**. But before we move on, let's evaluate the finer point of **how** *we are* **actually** *born again* in this **1 Peter 1:3** passage:

"Since you have **purified** your souls (by way of Christ) in **obeying** the truth (of God's Word) **TROUGH** the **Spirit** in sincere love of the brethren, love one another fervently with a pure heart, having **been born again**, not of corruptible seed (our flesh) but incorruptible, **TROUGH** the **Word of God** which lives and abides forever."

I am sorry to tell you that **none** of us can do this by, and *through* ourselves outside of His Spirit, because the new birth, can **only** come from God when we meet **all** of His conditions, spelled out not only here, but throughout His Word, as has been covered here—and scripturally proven so far. Also, for the simple reason that salvation is **limited** to merely being saved *from the His wrath* to come.

Period, it's not more complicated than this.

Who are the Sons of God?

Why is it important to understand why **we must be born again**, as **1 Peter 1:23** clearly says, **through the Word and His Spirit**? Here is another truth bomb where the sheep have been misled by church teachings into thinking that by just "*believing*," they automatically become a child of God. But before you shut me off, **let's read what God has said** about this because religious bias, will always reject an *inconvenient truth*. And trust me, I myself *had a hard time* with it, until He presented His case in His Word.

We choose to forget that God chose, *out of the whole earth*, only *One man*, **Abram**, after He **wrote off** the rest of mankind in **Deut. 32:7-9** (below), except the seed of Shem. Nor the fact that, as **Rev. 20:8** tell us that a group of **believers** who entered the Millennial Kingdom and lived in it, for as long as a *thousand years*, whose "number is like the sand of the seashore."

This *very same people* who had lived in **a perfect world** under Christ Jesus as King, *rebelled and attacked* the Heavenly Jerusalem *to remove* Him from His Throne as King of the World.

So, the question is, *would a **real** born-again son of God do this*?

Let that sink in.

How do we know all of these details? He tells us where it started in **Deut. 32:7-9**. These two verses read in Hebrew, as close as possible in English:

"When the Most High gave the nations their inheritance (*allotted* all the land of the earth **except the Holy Land** to them), when He separated [divorced] the sons of man (at the *Tower of Babel*)], He set the boundaries of the peoples according to the number of the *sons of God* (the **fallen angels** who became the false gods to the fallen humanity—**not** the asinine idea of the "theologians" who teach it as "the number of the *children of Israel*."). For the Lord's **portion** (the Holy Land) and **chosen share**, is His people; Jacob (Israel) is the *allotment* of His inheritance."

(see confirmation in **Acts 17:26**).

Just consider how low the spiritual IQ of these "theologians" are, trying to *divide 70 nations into 12*, the number of Jacob's sons. If it weren't sad, it would be laughable.

This is another religious misconception which, just like the belief that salvation and entering the kingdom are **one and the same**, and who think that by just "*believing*," one becomes a child of God as if by magic, comes from fertile religious minds from seminaries incubators. Not so, again, they are **two separate** things.

Here is what **God says** about **what is** the **requirement** is, to *be a son/daughter* in **Romans 8: 13-14**:

> "For if you are *living according to the* [impulses of the] *flesh*, you are going to die. But if [**you are living**] by the [**power of the Holy**] **Spirit** you are habitually putting to death the sinful deeds of the body, you will [really] **live forever**. For **all** who are **allowing** themselves to be **led by the Spirit of God ARE sons of God**."

And in **Matthew 5:9**:

> "Blessed [spiritually calm with life-joy in God's favor] are the makers and maintainers of peace, for they will [(through the Holy Spirit) **express His character** and] be called the *sons of God*" (see **John 12:36**; **Gal. 5:6**; **Gal. 4:5-6**).

This is what **He** has **declared** in His Word, I am just the messenger.

Prodigal Son's Lesson

Think about this in terms, and the context of the parable of the Prodigal Son, where after offending the father, he **separated himself** from him, but he never *forfeited* his sonship relationship, but it took repentance to regain that position again as a member of the family. However, do not lose sight that the father, once he came back, *did not say* to the returning son what he said to the **obedient** son: "Son, **you are always** with me, and **all that is mine is yours**." The younger son only got new clothes, sandals, and a ring signifying family affiliation. Our Lord Jesus is trying to tell us that there is a lesson in this parable about the nature of sonship and obedience.

His message is quite clear; sonship is a **CHOICE**. This young kid had a decision to make—do I live in this pigsty (the worldly life and/or my religion) **OR**, do I go back (*spiritually speaking*) to my roots, and be in the **presence of my father**? We can also see clearly that the father didn't scold or berated him for leaving home but showered him with love and celebrated his repentance and return. How grand is that? Nevertheless, I am only speaking in human terms in my understanding, **not** what it's going to be like in eternity, but I do know that **nothing** that is written in His Word, is just for window dressing, but for a **reason and a purpose**.

The Word and His Spirit

So, according to His Word above, if I have "**been born again**, not of corruptible seed (our flesh), but *incorruptible* **TROUGH** the **Word of God**," is there any other **argument against how important** it is to have a *thorough knowledge* of God's Word, or that, not having *our fellowship with the Holy Spirit* is something to casually disregard, and then not having consequences to face for this neglect?

Or for that matter, that **NOT** "**obeying** the truth (of God's Word) through the Spirit" will somehow, someway result in us *being* **born again** *by osmosis* inside a church, or that, *without* abiding in fellowship with Him **through** the Word and His Spirit have no consequences, given all of the scriptural evidence given so far? You judge, but I certainly don't think so.

He Alone Recreate Us

So, here we have self-evident proof positive for **any** Christian to confidently **know** and **discern**, whether one is, in fact, *truly*, "*born-again*," but only you and Him can be the judge of that. It's as simple as submitting to His Spirit's teaching, **using** His Word as **your Textbook**, not men's random thoughts on any given Sunday (see

Jeremiah 17:5 for the **consequences** of this choice), and He'll do the spiritual heavy lifting, as in **Genesis 1's** "God said"—and His Spirit acted—shows us the **How**—**Believe**, **trust**, and **obey** His Word, not religious voices, shows us the **When**.

Salvation is our divine launching pad to the **next level** to undergo into our born-again experiece that changes our daily living, with the **purpose** and **use** for **preparing** us for our future eternal life (**Philippians 2:12**; **Romans 6:22**; **Colossians 3:23**)—This is the structure, order, and the make-up of God's Redemption Plan capped by a **new birth**, which is *distinct* from the *salvation gift*. No diligence, no reward—it's His curriculum to graduate to our **inheritance as His priest** (**Numb. 18:20**; **Deut. 18:12**; **Hosea 4:6**; **Revelation 22:12-15**).

Our Inheritance is Earned

Today's religions peddle a mirage—programmed by "theologians" lacking biblical ground, or knowledge. Yet, Scripture reveals clearly, God's goal—**priesthood** via **Spirit-led Word knowledge** and lived (*demonstrated*) by our daily personal life, and in our dealings with our neighbor. But for the religious mind, it's too fantastic to fathom and means little; for those sensing a gap in their Christian walk, it's a springboard to rival the life of the many biblical characters through-out Christianity's history. The religious establishment **lacks** the Spirit's power and authority—only **personal fellowship** with Him delivers.

Scripturally Proven

Now that we have read and proved scripturally that this kingdom's inheritance is **not** part and parcel of our salvation, as is illustrated in **Rev. 22:12-15** in His own Words, it does take, however, His Spirit to reveal what has been carefully weaved and described throughout His Word about how we can receive it.

Nevertheless, for those who *may not be satisfied* with the current version of Christianity *as is*, this information, knowledge, and understanding can become a new starting point for an amazing experience with the Savior.

I know all this may sound incredible and even far-fetched, but as noted before, this cannot be described by words but **only lived and experienced** in real time, in one's life.

Our Responsibility

Be Careful Who You Listen To

In **Mark 4:24**, He places the responsibility about what and who we are to listen to, and places it squarely on our shoulders and not on somebody else's, regardless of who they are:

> "Then He said to them, 'pay **attention** to what **you** hear. By your **own** standard of measurement [that is, to the **extent** that **you** study spiritual truth and apply godly wisdom] it will be *measured* [back] **to you** [and **you** will be given even **greater** ability]—and **more** (knowledge and wisdom) will be *given* to **you** besides'."

The hierarchy won't highlight this path (**John 14:6**)—it threatens their power and control (**John 11:48**). Human nature resists disruption. Why's this vital? I'll explain this with analogies, wrestling spiritual truths into words. So, let me step aside off the path that we have been on, and explain to those who will act on all of this information why this is important not only to know, but to understand it.

Oneness With Him

This process of being **One** with Him is explained by Him in **John 17:22-23**:

> "I have **given** to **them** the **GLORY** and **HONOR** which You have **given Me**, that they may be **one**, just as We **are** One; I *in them*, and You in Me, that they *may be* **perfected** and **completed** into **one**, so that the world may know [without any

doubt] that You sent Me, and [that You] have loved them, just as You have loved Me."

This is confirmed in **Ephesians 4:4**:

"There *is* [only] **one body** [of believers] and **one Spirit**—just as you were called to **one hope** when called [to salvation]."

And in **1 Corinthians 6:17**:

"But the one who is **united and joined** to the Lord is **one spirit with Him**."

Now, keeping God's perspective of us being **ONE** with Him, do not miss the truth that the expression of, "that they **MAY** be **one**, and that they *may be* **perfected**," in **John 17:22** above, clearly indicates that this state of being, is **our choice** not His, as in "I **may** decide to be **obedient, or not**." The fact that we now have thousands of religious groups, and denominations of every kind, flavor, and color, tells us that the latter decision is the prevalent one, and not the former.

Motives Matter

One can, therefore, say that, when it comes to walk with His Spirit, it all comes down to what *our motivations* are, and what are our perceived benefits in our decision to follow *men*, versus those from **God** by following His Spirit (**Psalm 103:2**, and **116:12**).

That's the danger that too many Christian's face, who choose **to be one** with their chosen religion, rather than walk with His Spirit. For some reason these sincere people do not grasp, or get it at all, due to faulty teachings that, once saved, God's expectation is that *we do have to work out* our own salvation (**Phil. 2:12; 1 Timothy 5:18; 2 Timothy 3:17**), but rather to work hard, and pay heavily in "tithes," for the salvation preached by others according to their will, not His.

The fact that salvation ***only*** saves us from wrath to come at the end of the age, is lost in the cacophony of false teachings all over the religious world.

Work for the Whole Package

So, instead of working towards receiving the easy way salvation ending up spinning your religious spiritual wheels—getting nowhere close to where God wants you to be—choose to work for ***whole salvation package*** that **includes** an ***inheritance***, to fulfill **Eph. 3:16-19** in their ***own individual*** life so that, He can:

> "Grant you out of the riches of His glory, to be strengthened and **spiritually energized** with **power** **through** His Spirit in your **inner** self, [indwelling your innermost being and personality], so that Christ may dwell in your hearts **through** your faith. And may you, having been [deeply] rooted and [securely] grounded in love, be fully capable of comprehending with all the saints (God's people) the width and length and height and depth of His love [fully experiencing that amazing, endless love]; and [that you may come] to know [practically, **through** personal experience] the love of Christ which far surpasses [mere] ***knowledge*** [***without*** experience], that you may be filled up [throughout your being] to all the fullness of God [so that you may have the richest experience of God's presence in your lives, completely filled and flooded with **God Himself** (**none** of this is possible **through any** religion)]."

Saul's Lesson

Therefore, if we neglect to walk in the Spirit, we are no different than king Saul, who had been chosen to be king over Israel, but had no clue about His Law, that his calling as king, required of him to know, so that he would **not violate** God's commands, as explained to him by Samuel the prophet in **1 Sam. 15:22:**

> "Has the Lord as great a delight in burnt offerings and sacrifices As in ***obedience*** to the **voice** of the Lord (written to us today in

our Bibles)? Behold, to **_obey_** is better than sacrifice, And to **_heed_** [is better] than the fat of rams."

Let us also remember that God treated Saul **_the same as David_** because:

"Then it happened when Saul turned his back to leave Samuel, **God changed** (just as He did with David) **his heart**" (**1 Sam. 10:9**).

Today, He has already told us, His saints, what should be our only motive behind our service and obedience towards Him, in **John 14:15**:

"If you [**really**] **love Me**, you **_will_** keep _and_obey_ **My** commandments (**not** those from your religion/denomination and their man-made rules)."

This statement by our Lord is just to remind us what is, our own indicator and criterion to measure **our love** for Him, determined by the **_level of our obedience_** to Him and His Word in our daily life. This isn't meant to chide us, but to encourage us with His own Love for us, which to me, is still hard to fathom and comprehend, how such a formidable, magnificent, and beautiful God, can have such Love for our human race.

Religion's Drift

How did Christianity go so far astray over the past 1,800 years? The first step was the fact that a man-made religion, took the place of the spiritual worship that He described to the Samaritan woman (**John 4:23-25; 1 Cor. 2:13; 2 Cor. 1:12**), whether intentionally or not, it doesn't matter because had these men been **walking** with the Spirit back in the third century, this drift would have **_never_** happened.

Once these religious agents usurped the Spirit's teaching role (**John 14:26; 16:13**)—not ordained by God—most church teachings became mere words from man's, laced with opinions, personal beliefs, and traditions, not His Word—being that they are mostly preaching opinions, assumptions, and personal beliefs because it is not coming from His Spirit.

The proof is the pudding—all they did was to produce divisions, mediocrity, error, and self-delusion while burning at the stake alive, the real Christians. The sheep think that with creeds, doctrines of men, and dead works (**Hebrews 6:1**; **9:14**), that they are going to inherit the Kingdom, but in reality, all that they have done, is only *lose* their very prize they think they have (**Philippians 3:14**; **Colossians 2:18**), just as our Lord Jesus said about the Jews around Him in **Matthew 8:11-12**.

I pray that my readers will dig into all of these Scriptures—truth awaits. It's truly unfortunate that the sheep has bought into all this error, hook, line, and sinker, and have submitted themselves to this subtle deception that has kept them clueless and naïve about God's Truth, despite the warning found in **2 Corinthians 2:11** for us to:

> "Keep Satan from taking *advantage of us*; for we are not ignorant of his schemes."

Pastors Overstep

The overall religious result of these self-importance religions has been that of a mediocre scriptural education for the sheep at best, and a disaster at worst, based on their history of the last 18 centuries. All we can do is to pray for those with religious closed minds, blind spiritual eyes, and deaf ears. I hope to encourage them to search these scriptures—much of what they hear in churches is **not** the Word of God.

The tacit approval from the sheep, is what allowed these agents of religion, to presume to be the authorized "teachers" to the flock, contrary to His instructions in **John 14:26**, and **16:13**. The fact remains that they *took the role of theologians* as if they had been ordained, or authorized by God, to **replace** His Spirit (whether is being done maliciously or not, is irrelevant and immaterial).

Chapter Seven

Entering the Kingdom is Our Reward

Biblical Truth is by Revelation Only

There is Unity Only in the Spirit

Just like it was in Jesus' days, if one wants to *know Truth* today, one must abandon all kinds of *preconceived religious ideas* that have been taught, drilled, and inculcated, into the church going folk's consciousness without *any* <u>credible biblical authority</u> per **John 14:26**, and in **16:13**, or on *any spiritual basis*, as in <u>knowing God's thoughts</u> (**1 Cor. 2:11**; and in **2:13**) in order for me or anyone else to accept, and hold them to be, as being the true "representatives" of God by any religion or sect *beyond any reasonable doubt*.

Once one fully understands what the Author of the Word said to the Samaritan woman in **John 4:21-24** and *specifically* in **verse 24**:

> "God **is spirit** [the Source of life, yet invisible to mankind], and *those who worship Him* **MUST** (no "ifs, buts, or when's" here) <u>worship in spirit and truth</u>."

These words alone would alert anyone with simple, basic common sense, and logic, that **every Word of God** has a **spiritual**

essence, **root**, **and meaning** that **excludes**, and renders **any human being incapable to decipher them**, and be able to explain it to others, **EXCEPT** by the Spirit of God, its Author. Period, end of story!

We Can Hear Him Through Others

This doesn't mean that one cannot read and discussed it, but at its core, its meaning remains **personal** and *independent from the opinions of others*. God is free to send *anyone* your way if He finds a gap in your understanding that others have gotten from Him.

This is exactly the way He **designed** it and the **REASON** why He gave His Spirit to each one of those who answered His call. This is the message of **Ephe. 4:1-6**:

> "So I, the prisoner for the Lord, appeal to you to live a life **worthy of the calling** to which you have been called [that is, to live a life that exhibits godly character, moral courage, personal integrity, and mature behavior—a life that expresses gratitude to God for your salvation], with all humility [forsaking self-righteousness], and gentleness [maintaining self-control], with patience, bearing with one another in [unselfish] love (**John 13:34-35** and in **15:12-17** plus many others). Make every effort to keep the **oneness of the Spirit** in the bond of peace [each individual working together to make the whole successful]. There *is* [only] **one body** and **ONE Spirit**—just as you were called to one hope when called [to salvation]—**one Lord, one faith, one baptism, one God and Father** of us all who is [sovereign] above all [working] through all and [**living**] **in ALL**."

Considering the thousands of self-serving religions out there, is it starting to make sense now **why** there is **only ONE Spirit** assigned to teach **ALL** of those who have been *called*? Does it also now make sense that only those who *respond* to the call of the Spirit are the *chosen* ones (**Matt. 22:14**)? If it doesn't, then you **missed the point** of the whole story in the Old Testament about God **separating** the tribe of Levi, from the rest of the other tribes.

Our Temple Worship is Within Ourselves

But even more important for Christians today is their egregious dismissal of **John 4:21**:

> "Jesus replied, 'Woman, believe Me, a time is coming [when God's kingdom comes (i.e. when the Spirit comes to live in us)] and it's **already here**, when you *will worship* the Father **neither** on this mountain, **nor** in Jerusalem.'"

That is, in today's vernacular—woman, you will worship *neither* in the **Samarian Church**, **NOR** in the **Jerusalem Church**, or for that matter, in the catholic, protestant, Mormon, Baptist church, etc., etc.—ad infinitum.

Why is this so, where we **can't no longer hear** what Jesus is **really saying to us**, when we read his Word without the guidance of his Spirit?

Yes, it's so obvious it defies any explanation.

The Supremacy of His Spirit

As we begin to fully assess the true order and landscape of God's plan for **each one** of us, and it does, and will explain the **necessity** of having His Spirit as our **only** Teacher, Guide, Revealer (**John 16:13**)—Helper, Comforter, Advocate, Intercessor—Counselor, Strengthener, and Standby (**John 14:26**) that dwarfs anything than any religion can offer anybody who truly **wants to personally know** our Lord Christ Jesus. And as we are to find out now, why it matter to each individual who **answered** His call.

Citizenship or Priesthood?

His Reward for Faithful Works

Let me close this discourse by providing something for you to think about and consider, about the weight and ramification of the passage found in **Revelation 22:12-15**—study it **for yourself** rather than limiting yourself to what you have heard from your religion and *from others*. I have referenced this passage a few times throughout the discussion here.

So, let me lay out its compelling biblical reason, justification, and confirmation—its basis, and rationale that are behind our Lord's Words in this concluding chapter in the **Book of Revelation**.

But before we do so, we *must* first review what He reveals to us about the process of **our own *verdict and conviction*** at the Judgement Seat of Christ (**2 Cor. 5:10**; **1 Peter 4:17**) and it is found in **1 Corinthians 3:1-15**:

> "But each one must be **CAREFUL how** he *builds* on it (**YOUR** foundation, ***singular***, not plural as in you alone, ***not*** your church) for *no one* can lay a foundation (***not*** your religion or pastor) *other* than the one which is [already been] laid, which is Jesus Christ. But if anyone builds on the foundation with gold, silver, precious stones, wood, hay, straw, each one's work will be clearly shown [for what it is]; for the day [of judgment] will disclose it, because it is to be *revealed with fire*, and the fire will test the **quality** and **character** and **worth** of **each** person's **work** (the work, not your faith). If any person's work which he has built [on this foundation, that is, any *outcome of his effort*] remains [and survives this test], he will *receive a REWARD*. But if any person's work is burned up [by the test], he **WILL SUFFER THE LOSS** [of his **reward**]; yet he himself **WILL BE SAVED**, but only as [one who has **BARELY** escaped] through fire."
> (See **1 Cor. 3:8**; **Col. 3:24** [revealing **what our reward is**], and how you can **lose** it in **1 Cor. 6:9**. and in **Gal. 5:21**; and **2 John 1:8**).

This verse is all about Jesus' Judgement Seat (**2 Cor. 5:10**; **1 Peter 4:17**; **1 John 4:17**). It is in **this passage** of Revelation 22:12-15 where our Lord Jesus spells out **who are the ones who built** well on their foundation with *gold, silver, precious stones*, and who **did not**:

"Behold, I (Jesus) am coming quickly, and My ***REWARD*** is with Me, to **GIVE *to EACH*** one ***ACCORDING*** to the **merit of his deeds** (our earthly efforts of ***our WORKS*** and faithfulness in **response** to His Word). I am Alpha and the Omega, the First and the Last, the Beginning and the End [the Eternal One]. Blessed (happy, prosperous, to be admired) are those who wash their robes [in the blood of Christ by believing and trusting in Him—the righteous *who **DO** His commandments*], **so that *they* may have *THE* RIGHT *TO the Tree of Life* AND** may **enter** by the gates *into* the city."

Entering the Kingdom is Our Reward

These Words of His here, are the **definite and final** proof that one **must earn** the **Right** to have **access** to *Tree of Life*, **BUT**, to have this access, one **must be able enter** the City.

The Greek meaning of words here leaves no doubt about this whatsoever, and the fact that **we must earn our inheritance.**

"*May have*"—(in Greek: "**shall be**")— and—"*right to*" (in Greek: "**regal authority**, **crown**") signals **our** future inheritance [our priestly reward] **earned** in **this** life, **not the next** (**1 Corinthians 3:14; Philippians 2:12**). This **Revelation 22:12-15** passage ties the word "**right**"—(Greek: (*exousia*), **with regal authority**)—**what allows**, and **grants**, us to have **access** to the **Tree and City**—so, our priestly inheritance is **earned**, *not gifted.*

To "**Enter**" (**John 1:12; Romans 8:13-14**) is connected to **works**, and **not** to our **gift** of **salvation**, and neither one is linked to **faith.**

Merriam Webster dictionary defines the words of having a "right to," as something that you are **entitled to**, and as, "something to which *one has a just claim*," or as "something that one may properly receive **as due** to someone."

Needless to argue that **none** of these definitions, in any way, apply to God's *free salvation* gift that, again, is declared all over the N. T. books to be **totally free.**

Therefore, our inheritance isn't free like salvation, and His Word links it with works in **1 Corinthians 3:1-15** to receive it as

His reward—in line with the construction material one **chooses**, **not by Him** but by us, to build on our own foundation (**Matthew 7:24-25**), whether it be gold and silver, or straw, hay, and wood—it's **our** call, **not** His.

Our Deeds Do Follow

Can we find a second scripture that **confirms** that our inheritance **is earned**, not given as a free gift? Yes, and it's clearly connected to the subject matter that we are discussing here, and is in **Rev. 14:13**:

> "Then I heard [the distinct words of] a voice from heaven, saying, 'Write, 'Blessed (happy, prosperous, to be admired) are *the dead who die in the Lord* from now on! Yes, [blessed indeed], says the Spirit, so that they may **_rest_** and have relief from **their labors**, for **their deeds** [**works, things done**] **do FOLLOW** *them*'."

Thrown Out of His Presence, Not Into Hell

In **Matthew 8:12** we can see the **consequences** of not doing His expectation of working out our salvation (**Philippians 2:12; 2 Timothy 3:17**) while He was in heaven where, in the context of its original Greek language, it gives this passage, a whole new meaning:

> "**will be** thrown out into the outer *darkness* (in the Greek this word can be translated as "*obscurity*, or *shadiness* as compared to the bright light of the sun at noon of His Presence); in that place [which is **farthest** **removed** *from the kingdom* (not **sent** to hell)] there will be *weeping* [in sorrow and pain] and *grinding* of teeth [in distress and anger."
> (also, in **Matt. 22:13; 24:51, 25:20**, and **Luke 13:28**).

The Parable's Point

Let's pause here and analyze the *full context* of the passage and let it sink in.

Here is an unprofitable servant who has swapped his *eternal reward* for worldly living, and material trinkets—including a religious practice or belief, if you will. Now, does this description in **Matthew 8:12** sound to you, in context, like the phrase "*the farthest place* **from the kingdom**," as if someone were being sent to hell? Does the Bible imply anywhere, that God's Kingdom would have hell in its vicinity?

I certainly don't think so.

In contrast to the parable in **Matthew 13:38-50**'s weeds, who are going to be burned, **Matthew 8:12** is describing someone whose works were burned as described in **1 Corinthians 3:1-15** and his/her "*weeping* [in sorrow and pain] and *grinding* of teeth [in distress and anger]," is the reaction of a **saved person**, realizing that one has **only this life** on this earth to earn His Reward.

Such reaction as in "*weeping* [in sorrow and pain] and *grinding* of teeth [in distress and anger]," speaks volumes as to how amazing this reward must be.

Christ Jesus Does Not Obfuscate Nor Lie

If one allows this passage in **Revelation 22:12-15**, to saturate our understanding and consciousness, and let it sink deep into our heart to open our spiritual eyes, one cannot assent to any other explanation about what this **Revelation 22:12-15** passage is saying, and what it means. He is plainly telling us that the rewards He is **bringing** with Him (**Isaiah 40:10; 62:11; Hebrews 11:6**) are based strictly on the works we did for **the love** we have for Him. This is also detailed in the **1 Corinthians 3:1-15** passage as clear as crystal.

Is Jesus lying to us in **Revelation 22:12-15**, or is He telling us here that the reward of God's inheritance *is free*, like our redemption? Certainly not!

His language is clear and concise, **differentiating** our reward from His grace. The Bible is self-explanatory, is it not?

Eyes Wide Open

Furthermore, since Jesus' Words in this Revelation passage **is not** a misrepresentation, nor a lie, He is clearly saying here that the rewards He is *bringing* with Him (**Isaiah 40:10**, and **62:11**; **Heb. 11:6**) **are due** and **payable** to any saint **because** of their works.

I cannot overemphasize this fact to counteract the deception found in the teachings of the "Christian" religions that entering the Kingdom is part of our salvation—having been inflicted on the church attending sheep, **for centuries**.

The Lazy Servant's Weeping's Source

If we neglect His call to be His priest (read **Exodus 19:6**; **Hosea 4:6**, and others), and we miss building on **His** Rock foundation (**Matthew 7:24-27**) our spiritual house—then, the "weeping and gnashing of teeth," is the *natural result* of a **great loss**, not because being sent to hell—logic agrees. Since the biblical evidence points that certainly, **our works determine** our inheritance, our **choices** then, do bear eternal weight and consequences.

Now, how then are we supposed to respond to this revelation if we fail *to see, and understand* this, and still choose to neglect to do such work? Is loving our God, after His great sacrifice **bared by Him**, not us, and loving our neighbor as ourselves such a great burden on us? I think not!

One of many obstacles for the average church goer is not being capable to understand the *divergence* between the **two foundations** one can build upon, and the other, is that the outcome of whatever choice one makes, rest entirely on *our shoulders*. This is why He says from **Matthew to Luke**, "there **will be** weeping [in sorrow and pain] and grinding of teeth [in distress and anger." Simple logic tells us that this kind of response can only point to someone who's suffered *great loss*, not someone who is sent to hell, don't you think?

Priestly Choice

One last point, and I can only hope that you will think carefully about all of this, and consider that there **are eternal ramifications** about, once more, in **our choice** on which foundation to build (**Matthew 7:24-27**).

Does this sound repetitious? It better be, is that critical and important **to know**. Unlike the Levites, who were bound to serve in the wilderness, we get to choose on **which side** of the Heavenly Jerusalem we get to spend eternity—just the saved people outside Celestial Jerusalem, or as a priest within (**Exodus 19:6; Hosea 4:6**).

God leaves **this choice entirely** up to us—pray, seek confirmation.

He won't force or condemn to hell anyone for not seeking the priesthood office—He, like any father to a child, just offers the best that He has as a reward (**1 Corinthians 2:9**) for just being **obedient** (**John 13:34-35**; and **14:15**).

Parables' Disconnect

God will never obligate any of His children to do something they **don't want to do**, nor condemn one for electing to do something else. It's just a matter of whether the reward is **worth** chasing after once you know about it.

Moreover, another theme in which to deliberate, and reflect also on it, is, that **IF**—and that's a big **IF**—our *salvation and entering* the Kingdom of God, are one and the same—but they are **not**—then the biblical evidence shown so far, could be biblically **refuted** by anyone directly from our Bible—tried that myself and couldn't find any.

So, let's prove it by asking a simple question—how is it that our Lord, in *every parable* regarding *the kingdom*, He never **connected** it to salvation, and why is this so? It's not difficult to figure it out for the simple reason that in every Kingdom parable, He always **imply** that living and being in this kingdom, it's something that can be **purchased** (as in **buying** the land with the treasure in it, buying the pearl of great **price**, etc.).

What Religion Offers to the Uninformed

However, religion **does imply** that it takes the "sacrifice" of attending a church a couple of times a week, live a busy life dedicated to religious work, and living an average routine daily life that *adapts* to this world which, typically, **excludes** having God's constant fellowship with us 24/7, and in everything else one does and decides to do.

I have known this life because I lived it. And that, in living such mediocre Christian life, will, somehow, someway, **qualifies** one to receive His inheritance? To think this, in view of what His Word says, would be, all things being equal, **irrational**.

Scripture's Purpose

If practicing any religion **sufficed**, then why does the New Testament's alerts us (**Romans 15:4; 1 Corinthians 10:6**, and **verse 11**) that the Old Testament was **written for us** as examples and admonitions to **avoid** making the same errors that Israel did in the past? And if that's not credible, or realistic, in the face of the evidence presented here so far, then please, think about all of those religious Jews in the gospels who chose to listen to the rabbis and scribes, rather than Jesus *despite* of the *evidence* that Jesus was presenting to them (and to us today in His Word).

He demonstrated to them the works He performed (**John 10:37-38** and **14:10-11**) that He was, indeed, the Messiah and the author of God's Law through Moses, just as the prophets had foretold.

Unfortunately, for Christians today, without *even knowing it or realizing it*, they are making the *same mistakes*, through **unbelief**, just as easily as those Jews did, who perished in that desolate Sinai desert did, and it's **no different** than what those, equally religious Jews, did with Jesus as well.

Sin Redefined

Let's talk now about one of the most insulting errors present in all of Christianity today, such as the belief in religious circles, where they name *categories of* "*sins*," as in drinking alcohol, lying, or stealing, etc.—depending on which of their religious sensibilities is offended by individuals. But the Word defines *sin*, in *both*, the Hebrew and Greek, as an **offense** against God's **standards**. And what is His standard, unlike the Old Testament, for the New Testament saints? There is **ONLY ONE**, He tells us Himself in **Mark 3:28**:

> "I assure you and most solemnly say to you, **ALL** sins will be forgiven the sons of men, and all the abusive and blasphemous things they say; but whoever blasphemes against the Holy Spirit and **His power never** has forgiveness but is guilty of an **everlasting sin** (*singular*, **not plural**) [a sin which is **unforgivable** in this present age as well as in the age to come]."

He reconciled the world through Christ (**2 Corinthians 5:19**), taking away **all** of mankind's sins. **Psalm 103:12**, **Matthew 12:31-32**, along with **Mark's** verse above, confirming this.

Therefore, it is *crystal clear* that by **God's standards**, He will judge only **ONE SIN**—the rejection of Christ, by calling the Spirit a liar, because of their **unbelief** of His testimony about **who Christ Jesus is**.

God' Goal for His Church

In regards about our inheritance of God's Kingdom, let's just think about this in a different way—what was the end goal, God's Target if you will, after saving the Jewish slaves out of Egypt? It's the **SAME** for the N.T., as well, and that's easy to figure out, He tell us this in **Numbers 26:55**:

> "But the land shall be divided by lot. They shall *receive their inheritance* according to the names of the tribes of their fathers (tribal ancestors for the Jews and for us, the **Name** of Jesus)."

Oh, someone might argue, "this inheritance business, that's Old Testament stuff." Not so fast, because then one *has* to explain to me, **Acts 26:16-18**:

> "Get up and stand on your feet. I have appeared to you for *this purpose*, to appoint **you** [to serve] as a minister and as *a witness* [to testify, with authority,] not only to the things which you have seen, but also to the things in which I will appear to you, [choosing you for Myself and] rescuing you from the Jewish people and from the Gentiles, to whom I am sending you, *to open their [spiritual] eyes* so that they may turn from darkness to light and from the power of Satan to God, that they *may receive forgiveness and release from their sins*, **AND** an INHERITANCE among **those who** (is clear here that is **not** all, but **only** *those*) have been sanctified (set apart, made holy) by **faith in Me**' (faith *expressed* by our **obedience**)."

Here we see the division, and **difference** between **salvation**, given free through **believing** in the gospel, and an **inheritance**, **faith in Me**, and a reward for works, made of "gold, silver, precious stones, **not** of wood, hay, or straw" (**1 Corinthians 3:12**). Salvation is **only** the *forgiveness of our sins*, and it is free—the inheritance *requires* **sanctification** by **faith** (not merely **belief**) **in Jesus** (see **Matthew 8:11** and **22:12** among others)—as well as by our **obedience** in love (**1 John 4:19**).

Needless to say, this sanctification is needed **after** one's redemption which pre-qualifies **anyone** to start *working out* their salvation (**Phil. 2:12**) to receive His reward.

The Truth About Sanctification

I am sorry to say that the first reaction from most Christian who are well indoctrinated by tradition, and manmade doctrines, is that "*sanctification*" is the same as looking and acting pious, whatever that means in their eyes, doing church approved works, as well as doing whatever other duties as the denomination or group has determined.

In its simplest terms, biblically speaking, sanctification means our **willful separation** from anything that is worldly and **dedicate** ourselves to do *His will rather than ours*. We can see this in **Joshua 3:5**, **Isaiah 66:17**; **Joel 2:16**, and **especially**, **John 17:17** and many other passages.

But moving on, the other obvious conclusion is that this faith **has to be real**—the kind that achieves *obedience*, one that produces good works that are motivated by our **love for Him** because He loved us first (**1 John 4:19**).

This is what **James 2:19-26** is all about:

"You believe that God is one; you do well [to believe that]. The demons **also believe** [that], and shudder *and* bristle [in awe-filled terror—they have seen His wrath]! But are you willing to recognize, you foolish [spiritually shallow] person, that *faith without* [good] *works is useless*? Was our father Abraham not [shown to be] justified by works [of **obedience** which *expressed his faith*] when he offered Isaac his son on the altar [as a sacrifice to God]? You see that [his] faith was working **together with his works**, and as a result of the works, his *faith was completed* [reaching its *maturity* when he expressed his faith through **obedience** (to His Words)]."

Spirit-Led Living

By His Spirit Alone

Furthermore, in the Book of Zechariah, He makes it clear that **nothing** gets done unless it is *implemented, and executed* by His Spirit **IF**, we are **willing** to let Him participate in each of our individual lives. God yearns for us to **_know_** Him via His Word and His Spirit—no accident, but by design.

"Then he said to me, 'This [continuous supply of oil] is the word of the Lord to Zerubbabel [prince of Judah'], saying, '**Not** by *might*, nor by *power*, but **by My Spirit** [of whom the oil is a symbol],' says the Lord of hosts" (**Zech. 4:6**).

Wisdom's Source

God, in His infinite Wisdom (**Rom. 11:33**), has disclosed these things in His Word so that we can prove them for ourselves as **Prov. 25:2** points out, but this comes *only through* His established system of teaching by, and **through** His Spirit. The Psalms of King David are a rich source of counsel to experience daily life in the company of our Lord and Savior but, it all begins with having:

> "The [reverent] fear of the Lord is the **beginning** (the prerequisite, the absolute essential, the alphabet) of **wisdom**; A good understanding and a *teachable heart* are possessed by **all** those who **do the will** of the Lord; His praise endures forever" (**Psalm 111:10**).

Promises Fulfilled

He pledges this to believers who trust His faithfulness (**Psalm 25:12-14**):

> "Who is the man who fears the Lord [with awe-inspired reverence and worships Him with *submissive* wonder]? *He will teach him* [**through** His Word] in the way *he should choose*. His soul will dwell in **prosperity** and **goodness**, and his descendants will inherit the land. The secret [of the wise counsel] of the Lord is for those who fear Him, and He **will** let them **know** **His covenant and reveal to them** [**through** His Word] its [deep, inner] *meaning*" (see **Psalm 91:16**).

This promise is not for our next life's eternal plane (**1 Corinthians 2:9**)—it's for the here and now if *we act* on it in conformity with our calling.

Only He Can Open Our Eyes

Until one comes to accept the truth that He **alone**, is the only One that can open up our spiritual eyes, ears, and mind to the scriptures, and **not men** from any religious organizations, it's only then that He

will do for today's disciples, just what He did for the two disciples on the road to Emmaus, found in **Luke 24:25-27:**

> "Then **beginning** with Moses and [throughout] **all** the [writings of the] prophets, **He explained** and **interpreted** for them the things referring to Himself [found] in **all** the Scriptures."

Only He—not men or religion—**unveils Scripture**, and all it takes for us to trust and believe in His Word and promises. Outside of this, we're just hamsters in a religious cage—our Sundays listening is about man's wisdom, **not** the Spirit's Wisdom (**1 Corinthians 2:11**).

Stunted Growth

Only the Spirit bridges our Word ignorance through His ministry, and its consequences found in **Hosea 4:6**. Leaning on men, stunts the growth in the sheep—centuries of harm—selling their *birthright*, like Esau, for men's lentil stew of personal opinions, intellectual conclusions, and philosophy. That goes the same for the sheep, when they read their bible through their own intellect, for the same reasons.

The Roots of Unbelief

And why is this so? Well, **chapters 2**, **3**, and **4** in Hebrews diagnoses this problem as practicing the same **UNBELIEF** that the freed slaves out of Egypt *chose to have and exercise* in the wilderness once they were freed from their Egyptian way of life. Are there exemptions to God's rules? None—His character, faithfulness, and holiness **stand firm** (**Hebrews 13:8**):

> "Jesus Christ is [eternally *changeless*, *always*] the **same** *yesterday* and *today* and **forever**."

No Excuses

I dare say that in my experience and observations, that pastors, teachers, and preachers, **do not do** these things on purpose, or out of malice, but like the Jews in Jesus' time, only out of religious misrepresentation and misinformation, and their love for traditions however, for them, this was *not unexpected* even though, they **knew** the written Torah, but because they **did not** have His Spirit living within them (**John 5:38**; **6:53**; **16:3**), they, like today's church staff, *cannot perform* the Spirit's work.

In contrast, we Christians *do not have this excuse* either, nor justification for being plain Bible **illiterate** and *will be held accountable* (**Matt. 12:36**; **Luke 8:18**) about this, *not* in regard to our salvation, but for refusing to act on our **eligibility** to be His priest (**Hosea 4:6**). But, truthfully, very few religious representatives are *not willing* to teach this, if they are aware of it, nor buck the system out of their respect and fear (**John 9:22**), and compliance to religious rules and love of traditions (**Matt. 6:2**; **John 12:43**).

Nevertheless, it is clearly asserted in **1 Cor. 2:10-14**:

> "For **God** (not a man or religion) has **unveiled** them and **revealed** them to **US through** the [Holy] **Spirit**; for the Spirit searches all things [diligently], even [sounding and measuring] the [profound] depths of God [the divine counsels and things **far beyond** human understanding]. For what person knows the thoughts and motives of a man except the man's spirit within him? So also **no one** (ibid.) knows the thoughts of God **except** the Spirit of God. Now we have received, **not** the spirit of the world, but the [Holy] Spirit who is **from God** (ibid.), so that *we may know and understand* the [wonderful] things freely given to us by God. We also speak of these things, **not in words taught *or* supplied by human wisdom**, but in those taught **by the Spirit**, combining *and* interpreting spiritual thoughts with **spiritual words** [for those being guided by the Holy Spirit]. But the natural man does not accept the things [the teachings and revelations] of the Spirit of God, for they are foolishness [absurd and illogical] to him; and he is **incapable** of under-

standing them, because they are **spiritually discerned _and_ appreciated**, [and he is unqualified to judge spiritual matters]."

Just how much clearer can this establish that **man** is *incompetent and unqualified* to discern **spiritual** words and thoughts that **only** His Holy Spirit can? Is there any wonder then, why the vast majority of Christians are stuck in a permanent state of *spiritual infancy*?

True Maturity

We can conclude then, that it's not difficult to see where the real problem lies for these local churches but, in the final analysis, it's **NOT** what I, you, the sheep, the organized church, or the world at large thinks about what real Christianity actually is, but about what He has already **revealed** in His Word. I believe that the majority of the disciples and followers of our Lord Jesus after the resurrection, were **spiritually mature** being taught by God Himself through Jesus' Spirit, just as He said in **John chapter 17** and, unlike those slaves out of Egypt, they were *obedient* to His commands as Paul observed this in **1 Corinthians 2:6-7**:

> "Yet we **do speak** wisdom among *those spiritually* mature [believers who have *teachable hearts* and a *greater* understanding]; but [it is a higher] wisdom not [the wisdom] of this *present age* (found so often in Sunday sermons) nor of the rulers *and* leaders of this age, who are passing away; but we speak *God's wisdom* in a mystery, the *wisdom* once *hidden* [from man, but *now revealed* to us *by God* (not man, but *only through His Spirit* dwelling in us), that wisdom] which God **predestined** before the ages to *our glory* [to *lift us* into the glory of **His presence**]."

Beyond My Outline

As I now close this, I have to confess that, when He guided me to write about this theme, and proceeded to develop a mental outline about what I was going to write. However, once I started writing, He expanded this work beyond the scope of my planned one, weaving Scriptures in the **precise order** to give it its full meaning, and the authority of His Word behind it.

And so, I have also learned all of these insights along with you—me as I wrote it—you, by reading it in a new light of understanding. To Him be all the glory and praise for His wisdom and knowledge to elevate us to a new level of *fellowship* and daily living with Him, so that we can be effective in:

"Destroying sophisticated arguments and every exalted *and* proud thing that sets itself up *against* the [**true**] knowledge of God, and *we are* taking every thought *and* purpose captive to the _**obedience**_ of Christ" (**2 Cor. 10:15**).

With the ultimate objective:

"[that you may come] _**to know**_ [practically, through _**personal experience**_] the Love of Christ which far _**surpasses**_ [mere mental] _**knowledge**_ [_**without**_ the experience], that you may be _**filled up**_ [throughout your being] to all the _**fullness of God**_ [so that you may have the richest _**experience**_ of God's _**presence**_ in your lives, completely filled and flooded with **God** Himself]" (**Eph. 3:19**).

Epilogue

Shifting Horizons

Throughout this work, my boundaries kept changing with new insights and new disclosures about the extent and scope of God's redemption plan as revealed in His Word. As I progressed with this composition, new questions, and topics of possibilities unrelated to the theme at hand unfolded—this last section following, is an example of that.

Something Unheard Of

He is my witness that I wasn't thrilled to write again about subjects that I have written during the last 15 years, nevertheless, as new insights emerged about His distinctive and specific plan of salvation that I had never heard, or be discussed by any Christian teacher, scholar, or theologian in the past 50 years of being a practicing Christian. Therefore, I had to follow His lead and follow the scriptural path that He provided to me, that ended into this totally new work which, as far as I am concerned, I have never heard anyone who has a public name and dissemination platform, talk, teach, or even mention it at all.

Along the Roman Road

Having said that, let me focus back with my own purpose about this last work which might be my last, unless He has other plans since I have made Him Lord of my life. Initially, I thought this would consolidate all of what I have written in the last 15 years but, as I see it now, this is only another facet, of many others, of that amazing salvation diamond gem.

On my side of this equation, my desire is to impart what His Spirit has graciously revealed to me, and share with others as expressed in **Romans 1:11-12**:

> "I may ***share*** with you some spiritual gift, to ***strengthen*** *and* ***establish*** you; that is, that we may be mutually encouraged *and* comforted by each other's faith, both yours and mine."

His Purpose

This new information about the scope of His Master Plan of Salvation that you have just read, is ***entirely His work***, and I cannot take any credit for something that I absolutely know, it's impossible for me put together or conceive.

This new learning here, has in essence, become my own Pearl of Great Price that I wish, everyone else could come to possess it as well, but beyond that to understand it's amazing intricacy and the way it's weaved throughout His Word.

But what about His own motive to reveal this now, in these last days? I honestly do not know, other than everything He does, it's for a ***reason and purpose***. With the sheer number of scripture passages quoted throughout this entire work, I can only guess that it's given for the purpose that He tells us in **Isiah 55:11**:

> "So will My word be which goes out of My mouth; it will **not** return to Me void (useless, or without result), without **accomplishing** what **I desire**, and without succeeding in the matter for which I sent it."

The Dual Type Pattern

As one immerses into the amazing narrative of God's Word from the very beginning in Genesis, one picks up on the contrast between all of the protagonists of the redemption story—Cain and Abel, Abraham and Lot, Jacob and Esau, Jacob and Laban, Saul and David, and a few other minor actors along the entire Bible story.

So, this *contrast* also *glides* into the followers of our Lord Jesus Christ pointing to this division as well—the difference between a *disciple* and a *believer*, as presented in this work. It is not a surprise either and this fits right in, that along the whole story of God's redemption plan for humanity, this duality of commitment and faithfulness is also present in the New Testament Church.

With this as the background, one can start recognizing subtle lessons emerging all along the storyline from Genesis to Revelation. One of the first ones, not as black and white as in that of Cain and Abel, is the story in **Genesis 13:7-11** describing the end of Lot's relationship with his uncle Abraham. Every story in His Word has a *reason and a purpose* for being written for our *instruction and warning* as it was established at the beginning of this work.

Winning or Losing it All

Lot, clearly closer to his uncle than his own father, seems to have missed his uncle's dealing with this God over the years with him—a personal God, much different than the idols that his family worshipped in Canaan (**Joshua 24:1-2**; **Ezekiel 16:2-4**) and still failed to see the eternal value in Abraham's relationship with God despite seeing what God was *actively doing in his uncle's life*.

But when the time came to go his own way, he chose the temporal—Sodom seemed good to him to have a new beginning—and it was there that he lost everything—but Abraham's choice, on the other hand, allowed him to gain everything. The moral of this story is that an opportunity can be placed right in front of your eyes and still amounts to nothing by what's in our heart. However, this advantage and heritage in joining this amazing God, was not overlooked by Isaac, Jacob, Joseph, Daniel, and many other outstanding men of God who chose to obey Him, and contrasted with other characters such as Jacob's uncle Laban, and later his brother Esau, though blessed by their relationship with him, ended up with the same negative spiritual results as those of Lot's.

Two Sons, Two Paths

Then we have the parables of two sons that illustrates the fact that in God's family of saints, adopted through the shedding of the blood of His Son, there are family members with *two kinds* of character, attitude, and mentality, which can be described as the obedient, and the stubborn. The latter is illustrated by the prodigal son, and the former by his brother who chose to stay with his father.

In this case, the father could have easily refused and deny the younger son of receiving any inheritance (see **Hebrews 9:16-17**) because he had not died yet, but that was not the main point of the story that our Lord wanted to point out, nor about the *difference* between the two sons involved in the account, but much later, about the father's response to the obedient one, who was told, "Son, you are **always** with me, and all that is *mine is yours*," after the rebel repented and came home. Contrary to what we might believe, this is directly connected to the warning found in **Hosea 4:6** which is directed specifically to those stubborn family members.

The other pair of sons are mentioned in the parable where one son told his dad that he would obey him, and do the work asked of him, and did not do it, while the other told the dad that he would not obey him but later relented and did the will of his father. All of these stories are still lessons directed to us today which validates the premise that we started with, which is that they were written for our *instruction*, *example*, *warning*, and *admonishment*. By all means, **do not overlook** that the fathers of these sons allowed them to do **their will**, not theirs.

Doers, Not Hearers

So, what are we to make about all of this? Well, from my point of view, and as a human being, I have yet to know of *anyone who would enjoy the fellowship of strangers*, over that of a loved one, such as a wife, children, mother, father, or any other cherished person. Therefore, Our Lord's Word in **James 1:22**, resonates with the topic and theme of this work:

> "But prove yourselves *doers* of the Word [actively and continually **obeying** God's precepts], and not *merely listeners* [who hear the Word but fail to **internalize** its meaning], *deluding* yourselves [by *unsound reasoning* **contrary** to the truth]."

Therefore, I am fully persuaded that our Father's motive behind this treatise is to make possible for anyone to know these things, and be able to make a quality, informed, and *biblically based election* as to which path is **the better choice**, rather than keep pursuing a trail based on the opinions of others, and not that of God's Spirit, who, in choosing their own way, will always be susceptible to misinformation, misrepresentation, and deceptive teachings, that are conducive for the uncommitted, to remain *uninformed*, if not *ignorant* about His Word.

Afterthoughts

For Those with Curious Minds

Spirit's Link

Have you ever wondered how our Father connects His Spirit with ours to establish a communication link, or a direct transmission channel, or even telepathy, if you will, with a specific frequency that is tuned to *each one of us*, so we can receive all of His thoughts and instructions—as restricted to us, as that of a radio station to connect with our mind and soul?

Throughout the Old Testament, patriarchs and prophets had clear and direct transmission channel with God.

I have experienced some of this, and I can definitely say that it is not in an audible way, but rather in the form of a whole thought as in a telegram, that I know are not coming from me. That's about as clear as I can describe it, and it took me quite a while to be able to distinguish and identify it as His, not mine. I can also definitely tell you that He uses His written word as a sort of His spoken language to us.

As these thoughts and revelations were developing themselves in me some ten years ago, I chalked them up to random thoughts, "hunches," and luck—some of them prevented serious accidents, and in my younger years from near-death incidents, or from disastrous outcomes—until I discerned that He was behind every unforeseen event and due to my ignorance about His ways and Word, I never had the chance to thanked Him for saving and protecting me.

A Possible Explanation

For those who like to study and to know, and keep up with the latest technological advances and trends, there has been, in the scientific medical community, a great health concern about the rolling out, and in current use now, the new 5G wireless communication system because, in more than a 1000 different studies, they have shown that EMF—in this wireless wonderland world in which we now live— has had various negative effects on the human cells and well-being where, by comparison, let's say, if one is listening any FM radio band, you are only being exposed to a signal that is only 98 MHz, **BUT**, on the other hand, when one is using a cell phone broadcast, whether is Bluetooth, or 2 GHz, 3 GHz, 4 GHz, and currently, 5GHz, we are talking being exposed to a **5 BILLION** frequency cycles **per second**, without even discussing the implications of the planned future use of higher transmission power levels of 6GHz, and even 10GHz currently in China.

Our DNA as an Antenna?

In 2011, Martin Blank and Reba Goodman published a paper where there is compelling evidence that our DNA potentially could be a *fractal antenna*—I highly recommend that you take the time, and research the Mandelbrot Set, and Fractal Structures that was recently re-discovered by an IBM research engineer, Benoit Mandelbrot in 1980—It's worth your time because it displays, not only a *visual beauty* of God's infinite wisdom and mathematical perfection, but it will also help you understand better, what I am about to share with you.

In order for a smart phone to receive all types of wireless frequencies whether it be LTE and 3G, like in Costa Rica when I am there, or 5G when I am in Arizona, your phone has a *fractal antenna* inside of it, in order to be able to operate and receive any type of cell signal of any strength that's available in your immediate area, or anywhere else in the world.

The Wonder of Our DNA

You see, **each one** of our body cells have our DNA stored in them in a compacted ball, which is known as a "*fractal globule*," with the characteristics and attributes where the DNA strands are tightly coiled like a ball of yarn, but it unwinds as easily as a memory wire, or a garden hose would straighten out when pulled off from a wall. If one understands the nature of antennas and the lengths needed to receive and send a transmission, the property of these globules would indicate an ability to receive the entire range of every transmission available in the universe, where *low frequencies* need a *long antenna*, but for the *ultra-high frequencies*, it must be a *truly short one*.

Obviously, this is a new field of science that we know little about, or whether these globules are able to pick up wireless transmission is yet to be discovered, and if they are—well, I don't think that we would be told about it because of the obvious military applications and implications. However, the damage to the human DNA that these ultra-high frequencies is real, and has inflicted in many people, real genetic and/or human cells damage, but that's outside our discussion here.

Unseen Impact

Since it is now known that exposure to these ultra-high frequencies have broken the strands in our physical DNA, it indicates that fractal globules may be, like, the fractal antennas in cell phones, capable of receiving these ultra-high frequencies as well, that potentially are inflicting damage on our body cells. As usual there will be a lot of controversy between the benefitting parties and the medical community and eventually, money and profit will win the argument, and show that there is nothing to worry about, "nothing to see here, move on," and go on to the 6G and beyond with cell phone frequencies.

Unfolding Answers

It has been my experience that as if, by "coincidence," new information comes my way magically that answers questions that I pose to Him. I have always been curious about the why and the when—all of what we see unfolding in this world, and by extension, this universe—it all began, and why. Deep inside, I know that nothing happens by chance and independently from other occurrences and events. I feel the need to understand my existence and role I play here, my immediate surroundings, and society at large.

Of course, if one believes that out of chaos came and amazing order through this whole creation, then, indeed, ignorance is bliss. How I am connected with Him through His Spirit and Word, was one of those questions to understand how I relate and interact with the outside world I am living in.

Fulfilling our Destiny

You see, as we establish this fellowship bond with Him, it is essential to *appropriate and utilize* His **power** (**Matt. 28:18; Luke 10:19; 2 Cor. 13:10**) that He has freely given to us—despite being and living behind enemy lines—and fulfill, with *His approval and total support*, the **charge He gave all of us** in **Genesis 1:26**:

> "Let Us (Father, Son, Holy Spirit) make man in Our image, according to Our likeness [not physical, but a **spiritual personality** and moral likeness]; and let them have **complete authority** over the fish of the sea, the birds of the air, the cattle, and *over the entire earth*, and over *everything* that creeps *and* crawls on the earth."

We can readily see in this **proposal and design** that to fulfill this plan, which **requires** a *resurrected and reborn spirit* from the spiritual death that Adam bequeathed to his posterity.

But not only this, Christians seem to have lost sight that, in losing our **spiritual connection** with God in that Garden, we also have **lost all** of His Wisdom as well, but true to His promises He tells us that He has restored that to us if, and once we are connected with His Spirit, and it's found in **James 1:5**:

> "If __any__ of you **lacks wisdom** [to guide him through [**every**] decision or circumstance], *he* is to *ask* of [our benevolent] God, who gives to **everyone generously** and without rebuke *or* blame, and it **will** *be given to him*"
> (see **Matt. 7:7; Ephe. 3:20**).

His Work is Already Completed

He also promises that *He is the One* who will **complete** it in us, not ourselves, nor **any** *church or religion* one chooses to practice, while we are on this earth. He says this as much—being that **my efforts** are neither involved, nor required in *any* capacity—in **Philippians 1:6**:

> "I am convinced and confident of this very thing, that He who has begun a good work in you, __will__ [continue to] **perfect** and **complete** it, until the day of Christ Jesus [the time of His return]."

If we understand the scope and scale of what He is telling us here, then one can't appreciate **1 Corinthians 13:10**:

> "But when that which is complete and perfect *comes* (our rapture), that which is **incomplete**, and **partial** will pass away."

Does DNA Has a Role in God's Communications?

Even though the function of fractal globules—our DNA's coiled marvels hints to be a potential spiritual antenna, this is still an open question in the scientific community. I did inquire of Him to give me some insight about the subject, and random thoughts did come through. Still, take this rejoinder with a grain of salt, as just my own *personal* opinion and view, where our ability to communicate with Him directly, is through our DNA—if and when you really analyze the nature and complexity of it—just like the patriarchs, prophets, and priests demonstrated that clear connection with Him.

Nevertheless, we can jump to the conclusion that anybody can do it at will. Common sense tells us that any communication device we have invented has a protocol in order to use and works according to its design.

His Way or The Highway

It shouldn't be surprising then that such a communications protocol would be present in His system of transmission as well. Just like those Bible notables of old, this is possible **only** when we do it **His way** (**Joshua 1:8-9**; **Matt. 6:33**), not ours. This hypothesis may explain the question many have asked as to why, the Covid 19 vaccines (once one is well informed about them), contain components in its formula that are designed to **alter** our DNA.

Coincidence? I think not!

I can't biblically prove our DNA's communication role, but circumstantial evidence, if not logic suggests it's a spiritual antenna—open to both bloodlines upon this earth—for God's children, and for those who choose the evil one's bandwidth, as history, and the daily news prove. Nevertheless, Christians alone are the only ones that can tune to His exclusive frequency via the Holy Spirit using our fractal network—something that is beyond any human comprehension as to how it works.

Religion's Disconnect

It is a given that we are a spirit, living in a physical body, and that religious institutions in contrast—none of them are living things, and therefore, they, as *inanimate* bodies, cannot be connected to Him in any way, shape, or form, and by **their choice** to be *divided*, rather than **united**, contrary to His will, is good enough proof for my, that *they don't have* **any** *access* to God's system that would give them **any credibility** to be speaking for Him.

These doctrinal divisions that are totally against His Church design and order and are confirmation that they lack *any standing or authority* from Him, to be in front of those called sitting in pews, as representing or doing what God *did not call them to do*. God did not give us His Spirit just for us to bench Him from His assigned work.

It is clear then, *who* is behind these institutions, discords, and rifts sown into every Christian religion—undoubtedly, at this level of deception, the devil has indeed gummed up the works of Christianity with these divisions, but he has **not conquered** the true Body of Christ within this network of denominational churches, according to the words of our Victor in **Matthew 16:18**:

> "And I say to you that you are Peter, and upon this Rock (**Christ**, *not Peter*, whose name in Greek means '*stone*,' not rock) I will build **My church**, and the gates of Hades shall **not** prevail against it."

Blind Guides

So, it is clear to me that, this being the case, it's easy to figure out, from where, and from **whom** these religious *splits and rivalry* originated, and my firm belief that they are still being **influenced** by the same spirit that deceived Eve. These rifts are nothing more than the old tactic of "Divide and Conquer," and boy, has the devil vanquished with these manmade institutions, but in no way **still able** to defeat those *who choose to walk with His Spirit*.

Now, for the religious doubting Thomas, who might be spiritually weak and easily deceived, this might be seen as something unconceivable because they might be deficient in their own level of **belief**, and thus, are unable to experience **Romans 15:13**:

> "May the God of hope **fill you** with all joy and peace in **believing** [through the **experience** of your faith] that by *the power of the Holy Spirit* (**not** your religion or denomination), you will **abound** in hope *and* overflow with **confidence** in His promises."

This state of affairs in the Christian church world of today, truly confirms the veracity of our Lord's Words in **Matt. 14:15**:

"Leave them alone; they are blind guides [leading blind follow-ers]. If a blind man leads a blind man, both will **fall** **into a pit** (see **Isaiah 42:16**).

True Fellowship

On the other side of this spectrum, we find Christians who *are willing to build their spiritual house* on the Rock, obeying His words found in **Matthew 7:26**, with a *predictable outcome* found in **2 Corinthians 13:11**:

> "Finally, believers, rejoice! Be made **complete** [**be** what you **should** be], be comforted, be like-minded, live in peace [enjoy the spiritual well-being experienced by believers who **walk** closely with God]; and the God of love and peace [the source of lovingkindness] **will be** with you."

Isn't this **exactly** what every Christian I know of, wants to have and feel again? That joy when we first came to Christ, but what has happened for all these centuries? Yes, they got stuck in a religious rut against His will, that He warned us about in **Galatians 5:9**:

> "Now, however, since you have come to **know** [the true] God [through **personal** experience], or rather to be *known by God*, how is it that you are **turning back** again (read **Exodus 14:12**; and in **32:23**; and **Num. 14:4**) to the *weak* and **worthless** elemental principles [of **religions** and philosophies], to which **you** want to be **ENSLAVED** all over again?"

Insulated by Faith

Therefore, we can all see that unless one *lives*, and *experiences*, this constant spiritual fellowship with Him, and not by one that is super-ficial and man inspired, that we might just be imagining through our hearing, by other human beings *who have no skin* on the game of our eternal destiny. No one *can* experience this personal oneness in real time, **24/7**, except us and not through an outside religious agency, given that they **do not** possess the **power or ability**, nor take the place and ministry His Spirit.

As a Christian, I am totally persuaded that my station of being born again, **insulates my DNA** from any interference, contamination, or corruption by anything that this world with its religion's institutions and government agencies, have to offer, or throw at me. This is also true for *any* other born-again Christian if *they walk* closely with their God (**Micah 6:8**) and are also in agreement with His Words (**Amos 3:3**).

I also believe that I am exempt from any harm, damage, or disruption from today's new communication technologies, which have the potential to be used by the enemy to *mentally influence* people, which may explain the current insanity that you see all around us here, and in the entire world at large.

The Coming Tribulation's Risks

There is a lot more that can be said about this, and how this spiritual connection with God will play a role during the tribulation where many, many, *misinformed and deceived* Christians will be misled into false doctrines, and end up being **left behind**, but not lost unless, they cross God's **REDLINE** of accepting the antichrist's mark on the hand or forehead, as warned in **Rev. 14:9**:

> "Then another angel, a third one, followed them, saying with a loud voice, '*Whoever* worships the beast and his image and **receives** the mark [of the beast] on his forehead or on his hand, he too **will** [**have to**] **drink** of the wine of the wrath of God, mixed undiluted into the cup of His anger; and he **will be** tormented with fire and brimstone (flaming sulfur) in the presence of the holy angels and in the presence of the Lamb' (Christ)."

This angel is not warning the *lost* people on earth—that's a given—since they are already done for, finished, and destined only to destruction (**Isaiah 34:5**; **Rom. 9:22**; **2 Peter 3:7**), but for only those who are still sitting on the fence in the midst of the tribulation.

It won't surprise me at all that many Christians will be left behind because they weren't **ready to meet** Jesus at the rapture of the Church (**Matthew 24:42-44; 25:10-13; Luke 12:35-40**).

Deception's Trap

Most Christians in the churches end up hearing and believing the same things that their pastors and teachers believe, say, and teach, including the errors they preach, because they were trained first in seminaries (monasteries for Catholic priests), where their doctrines were crafted, and second, because these errors filtered down to those sitting in the pews accepting and considering their words as being the "Word of God" through their lips.

Jesus warned us about this danger in all the gospels, but unfortunately, most Christians believe they are safe from deception, just like those religious Jews who fell into their own religious error when He was here.

There is a *reason* **why** He starts His warnings in the prophetic chapter in **Matt. 24** with the words: "**Do not be deceived**." Why would that be so, one might wonder? Well, because unless one does *due diligence* in *listening* to His Spirit only, and *obeying* His commands in His Word, then **every** promise in it, whatever they may be, **remains** *just a promise* until you **meet** all of His conditions for receiving them.

Therefore, one can only conclude that, given God's instructions on *how we are to live* our Christian lives after our salvation—from His perspective—then, if all it takes is to "*believe*" then, **adding 27 more books** to the Old Testament and the Gospels is totally **unnecessary**, would it not?—this is no different than when His people decided to replace Samuel (a **symbol** of the Holy Spirit in us) as discussed earlier.

However, if you decide to ally yourself with the religious establishment, as thousands Jews did in Jesus' time, then I would suggest reading **Jeremiah 17:5** about the consequences in trusting and relying on man.

This decision of doing just that, places a professing Christian in open rebellion and defiance of God's method, design, and order of business in His Church, and its mode of operation, not on those of any particular religion or denomination.

He is the Only Voice

The simple fact is that they *do not speak* on behalf of God but simply represent and peddle the beliefs and traditions of their own sect or denomination, rather than basing their claims strictly and **exclusively** on what God has already **declared** in His Word.

And what is the primary declaration of His Word regarding His Church? Well, we have already established the premise that God has ordained, designed, and prescribed that He, and **He alone**, is the **sole Teacher and Disciple of His sheep**, and if that is not good enough for you, then, good luck with your choice!

I hope that many of my readers will understand that, without **knowing** His Word, walking with His Spirit, and without **obedience**, living the *true Christian life*, as He planned and designed by Him for us, is not only *unattainable*, but *impossible* to accomplish.

Before responding to the Gospel Message in the summer of 1975, I lived a conventional and worldly life where everything in my daily life was "relative." I was the sole arbiter and judge of what is right or wrong in this world. At 18 years old, I lost my early year's attraction to the national religion of Nicaragua, and stopped going not only to church, but also rejecting their teachings about the existence of a higher being that demanded subjection to their religious God. However, in September 1974, I witnessed the birth of my first daughter and was mesmerized by this amazing miracle of life. This stunning work of creation instinctively pointed to me, about the existence of a great Creator whom I did not know, nor understand. This event was my own personal "Road to Damascus" experience and revelation, sadly, it only lasted just a few days. As the saying goes, out of sight, out of mind. But, what I saw that day, paved the path that led me a year later, to one night in Boise, Idaho, and to my salvation.

As I walked in my own manufactured faith that I thought I possessed, it seemed that all roads from that first day onward, always led to a church—in my case, to several different denominations—looking for a "missing link" that would fill the remaining vacuum I felt inside of me. Despite the randomness and uncertainty, I was hearing in those church teachings, which only casted doubts about those who were presenting themselves as "speaking for God," it did not match the God that I was seeing in my Bible. It took a few years of practicing the church phase that every Christian must go through, before realizing that something is lacking from what it's heard from pulpits, as compared to what I was reading in His Word. So, I endeavored to seek and find the not-so-obvious reasons of this divergence between what the denominational clergy believes and teach, and what is written in God's Word for all to discover according to Proverbs 25:2.

Through the years, I studied the Word of God as explained in this work, and realized that God is not interested in what church one attends, nor what is the pastor's opinion about what he "thinks" His Word means, or says, since only God can reveal it to each of His children, according to 1 Corinthians 2:11. All He ever desires is to have a personal, intimate relationship between Him and His child, the same one that Christ Jesus had with Him—which is personal and unique as the one we have ourselves with our earthly parents. He is only interested about instructing us how to live our life on this earth, and how through obedience, He can fulfill His promise of a John 10:10 life, which is true now in my own personal life, but with anyone else who dares to believe and trust His Words.

My search for answers and insights that He has provided me, have helped me to find a deeper, richer, and more meaningful daily life by connecting directly with Him and not trough a third religious party with no skins in the game of life.

"Knowing His Word — Faith for the End Times, is not preaching, nor a how-to book, but my evolution in discovering biblical truth that requires the readers to participate themselves by researching every scripture quoted, and dig deep into, not only His Word, but in their own heart, using the biblical tools that He has already listed and provided throughout His Word to find Real Truth, not a religious one. His Word, designed to be taught only by His Spirit, in lieu of His physical presence as with His disciples, is the only trustworthy teaching method and testimony for His children, who have come to the realization that nobody needs a middleman between them and their Heavenly Father as affirmed in 1 Timothy 2:5. The role for a pastor and a church, is to be only an assistant, tutor, mentor, and cheerleader for the benefit of our own progress and spiritual growth to develop a deep, meaningful relationship with Him. It's all about Him, and none of us.

www.ingramcontent.com/pod-product-compliance
Lightning Source LLC
Chambersburg PA
CBHW030221140626
46545CB00011B/583